His Precious Cargo

EMPOWERING PARENTS, CHANGING GENERATIONS

His Precious Cargo

Mary Catherine R. Ard'is

His Pen

His Pen, LLC
Tallahassee, Florida

Copyright

His Precious Cargo:
Empowering Parents, Changing Generations

by Mary Catherine R. Ard'is

Cover design by Lisa Hainline

Interior design and editing by Edie Glaser

ISBN: 978-0-9852007-0-1

CONTACT PUBLISHER

HIS PEN, LLC
P.O. Box 5034
Tallahassee, Florida 32314

Acknowledgments

To Father God, thanks for always being right here with me in my life, You are truly my ABBA.

Dez, beloved husband, confidant and love of my life: Thank you for always being a sounding board for everything I do.

"Mom" Sybil Mobley, you kept saying, "Mary, you have got to write the book on raising children because of how you and Dez are raising the four guys." Well, I finally did it! Thanks for your love and encouragement. It means a lot coming from you!

PeriSean Hall: Thanks for trudging through the manuscript, making me think, and come out of the box. You said go deeper in conveying my message. I did! You are a blessing.

Johana-Marie Williams: Thank you for lending your expertise in Creative Writing in doing the last proof read for this project. It does pay to always have many sets of eyes upon your writings to catch things that we who look at it everyday miss. God bless you in your endeavors as a writer.

There are people whose paths divinely cross for such a time as this, and so is the case of my "California Connections." This was one of those "not by power, nor by might, but by My Spirit says the Lord of Hosts."

Kathi Macias: You were divinely chosen to be the main speaker at our Writers Summit 2007 and has since remained a loyal friend and sister. My heart overflows when I think about how you were constantly encouraging me since day one. You gave your literary expertise and gifting to spend a day pouring over my manuscript. I appreciate your time, your effort, and your gift to me.

Lisa Hainline: I told Father God that I was not going to budge until He gave the green light on who to use to get the book cover created, and all I can say is Wow!!!!! Look what happened to a picture and how we met. God is so awesome because He gave me another spiritual daughter in the process. Keep the heart for our Lord and keep listening to Him and allowing Him to create through you the most beautiful and inspirational work.

Edie Glaser: What can I say my sister! I had to buckle down and listen to sound wisdom concerning the final edit and formatting, what is called book design. Thank you for keeping me centered on the point of writing to make it clearer. I got it!!! (smile) and it will go on through future books I am writing. I've gained another sister and friend in the Lord. Agape and Shalom to you!

From coast to coast in the states and from nation to nation, we say a hearty thank you to all of the village that extended favor from Father God throughout the raising of our precious cargo!

Dedication

This writing comes from the Father's heart through the pen of a ready writer. I honor Him for who He is. I love You, Lord—You are so very precious and such a blessing to me. I thank You, Holy Spirit, for guiding me through Your writing. I give it back to You!

To my precious sons, Dezmond Doron and Dominick Jabari, and to my nephews/sons, Joshua Allen and Jacob Michael, you are now like an olive tree planted in the courts of our Lord. Extend your roots so that they become immovable and steadfast in Him. Remember to put Father first in everything you do through our Lord Jesus, and Holy Spirit will forever guide your paths.

> Lean on, trust in, and be confident in the Lord with all your heart and mind and do not rely on your own insight or understanding In all your ways know, recognize, and acknowledge Him, and He will direct and make straight and plain your paths (Proverbs 3:5-6).

May He bless you with every Word in the first chapter of Ephesians, walking in divine alignment with and before the Lord in everything you do. Your Pop and I love you always!

Author's Message

Father God is looking throughout the earth to find daddies, pops, and fathers; mommies, moms, and mothers. who share the desires of His heart.

The Father's heart says, *"My people perish for lack of knowledge and I long to empower you to raise your sons and daughters according to My Word by My Spirit."*

By His Spirit, God empowers parents with knowledge of how to raise godly children. "Knowledge" comes from the Hebrew word *yada,* which means to know, without ignorance, to discern, to perceive, cunning, declare, respect, skillful, to know by observing and reflecting (experience with the senses by investigation and proving).[1] I'm not speaking of scholarly knowledge and neither is our Father. We are speaking of the type of empowering knowledge that only comes from God through a relationship with the Father through His Son. He gives us His moral and legal power as well as His divine and official authority because He is the great I AM, the Creator who is all-knowing and all-powerful.

Ability, enablement, permission, educating, resources, guidance, godly wisdom—they are all at our disposal whenever we need them; all we have to do is ask for and walk in them. We can change generational problems simply by walking in the way of the Lord as we train our children. I know this to be true because my husband Dez and I received empowerment from Father to achieve the raising of godly sons. It took transforming (renewing) our minds and hearts by His Spirit and following Him (His leading and direction).

> For I know the thoughts and plans that I have for you, says the Lord, thoughts and plans for welfare and peace and not for evil, to give you hope in your final outcome. Then you will call upon Me, and you will come and pray to Me, and I will hear and heed you, Then you will seek Me, inquire for, and require Me (as a vital necessity) and find Me with all your heart" (Jeremiah 29:11-13).

The heart of our Father is one of unconditional love, prayer, and justice with a realization that our Lord is holy, righteous, and His ways are just and pure. He needs parents that will train up His little ones to always put Him first, knowing that even before parents—He is; before grandparents—He is; before church—He is; before everyone and everything—He is.

The Truth is that Father will always love your children more than you do; He knows everything about them, and He will always be there for them. The earlier our children learn this truth, the sooner they will be able to tap into His love and direction for their lives.

I am honored, humbled, and thrilled that He taught us how to parent with His Heart in us, and He wants you to know how to parent with His Heart also. Yet, parenting is filled with challenges because parents must accomplish their duties working against the wiles of this world. Go against the normal in the eyes of the world to produce the normal in the eyes of Father, and allow Father to teach you by His Spirit how to parent.

Remember, "Unless the Lord builds the house they labor in vain those that build it." In Psalm 127:1, the word "house" in Hebrew also means family, and/or descendants. So we could read the passage as, "Unless the Lord builds the family they labor in vain those that build it." What a thought!

Let us pray:

FATHER GOD, in the name of Yeshua (Jesus Messiah), I thank you for touching and circumcising the heart of everyone who reads this book. Father, I thank you for revelations coming from Holy Spirit as they read the pages that follow, making your teachings for each parent clear and simple. I thank you for the wisdom, discernment, and knowledge which you impart to each one of them as they spend time with you.

Father, I thank you that you will give them the plan that You have for their families— plans of shalom (wholeness) in every area of their lives, to give them a hope and a future. I declare and decree that no weapon that is formed against them shall prosper, that they will rise up in the morning to seek Your Face to receive Your agenda for the day because the steps of a righteous man are ordered of the Lord.

I declare and decree that no plague or calamity shall come near their dwelling, that they will become doers of Your word not just listeners, that they will press in to You to hear Your voice, that still small voice bearing witness as they follow.

Father, guide, protect, and lead as no one else can so that these parents will raise champions for You and through You, for all vocations in life. Let them remember to give You all the glory, honor, and praise in the mighty name of Yeshua (Christ Jesus our Messiah). Amen (So be it).

Shalom,

Mary Catherine

Contents

Introduction

I ooked like an eggplant all covered up in a simple black abaya. In the sweltering heat of 110 degrees at the Riyadh airport, I rushed to get inside the car.

"Eshwaye! Eshwaye," I said to the tall, tanned man from Somalia.

"Madam, Madam, what do you mean?"

"Slow, slow," I replied, as I looked at my two young, exhausted sons. "You're carrying precious cargo!" We all laughed.

Whether we carry them in our wombs or hearts, prop them up on a hip, or nestle them close on our chest, who are our precious cargo?

The Old Testament writers used the Hebrew word for "precious" (*yaqar*) to mean precious; rare; excellent; weighty; noble."[1]

Cargo, however, is a much more practical than noble term. The famed wordsmith Noah Webster used the Bible as his source for defining English words and so shall I. In English, the word "cargo" means a load or a charge.[2]

A charge is a person or thing "committed, entrusted or delivered to another, implying care, custody, oversight, or duty to be performed by the person entrusted."[3]

Father God has given parents an enormous responsibility; He has given us a charge to train up our children according to His plan.

> Train up a child in the way he should go, and when he is old he will not depart from it (Proverbs 22:6).

In this Scripture, the word "train" is the Hebrew word *chanak,* which basically means to initiate/inaugurate/dedicate.[4] -As parents, we are set in place to unconditionally love, guide, protect, teach, and discipline our children so that roots are established in foundational truths from which they will never depart.

You may be thinking, *This isn't even remotely possible in my family, especially considering the dysfunctional home I came from.* I know what you mean. I really do. Consider this: both Dez and I came from single-parent homes. I had a beautiful, godly mother, but my parents divorced when I was in the fourth grade, and my mother practically raised the four of us herself. Dez didn't know his dad until adulthood, but he visited his grandparents every summer, and he still talks about the lessons that he learned from his granddad. Even with our fatherless upbringing, Father really blessed us when he allowed us to raise not two but four sons—the two we had biologically and our twin nephews, whom we became legal guardians of when they were fourteen, going on fifteen.

We could never underestimate the honor we felt in raising them up in the fear and admonition of the Lord. We as parents should want the same results. We fervently prayed that our teachings would bear fruit that remains long after they leave the supervision of our home. We lined up our hearts and minds with the heart of God and prayed His Word over each of our sons similar to this:

> Thank you Lord, for making our sons disciples (taught by You and obedient to Your will), so that they have peace and undisturbed composure. We thank You for fulfilling Your promise to establish

> them in righteousness (rightness, in conformity with Your will and order): to place them far from even the thought of oppression or destruction, so that they would not fear, and terror would not come near them" (adapted from Isaiah 54:13-14).

My God! What awesome promises Father makes in His Word that we can claim for our children. Yet, for them to become reality, our children need to see us running toward Him, walking in Him, and living for Him. Be established in Him (firm, set, faithful, stable, certain, prepared, immovable, anchored, and most of all enduring) at all times.

Children are great imitators and as parents we need to make sure that what they hear and see in the home lines up with the heart of God to prevent the arising of disrespect, and lawlessness toward parents, teachers, and civil authorities. We won't discuss the statistics; however, I have listed some web sites below for you to check out the state of the family and the urgent need to parent your children the way God intended. I list them because we forget that babies grow up to become adults who have babies, who become a part of these statistics in one form or another.

How do parents raise godly children, who raise godly children? I'm glad you asked! In the chapters that follow, I will share significant yet basic principles that have stood the test of time in the Ard'is household as we trained up, cared for, and dedicated our sons to the Lord. Grab a chair, bask in the sun with your ice tea, or snuggle in front of the fireplace with a good cup of coffee, but don't forget to grab your Bible. Listen intently for His voice, His leading, and His Word as Father speaks to you concerning your daughters and sons.

Learn more about the state of the family at

childstats.gov • childwelfare.org • barna.org • divorcerate2011.com

The humble child shall taste His grace
and the pureness of heart shall see His face.

~ Lila Carter Jones
Maternal grandmother
of author

Knowing the Father's Heart

In the Book that transcends time, events, and the modernization of the world, Father God relates to families from Adam and Eve to our Lord and Savior Christ Jesus. Like us, these families lived in His will and in disobedience; nevertheless, throughout every generation, His Word to the family never changes:

> The counsel of the Lord stands forever, the plans of His heart through all generations (Psalm 33:11).

It is our Father's heart for every generation to know Him and become complete in Him:

> Give ear, O my people, to my teaching; incline your ears to the words of my mouth. I will open my mouth in a parable (in instruction by numerous examples); I will utter dark sayings of old [that hide important truth]— Which we have heard and known, and our fathers have told us. We will not hide them from their children, but

> we will tell to the generation to come the praiseworthy deeds of the Lord, and His might, and the wonderful works that He has performed (Psalm 78:1-4).
>
> And His mercy (His compassion and kindness toward the miserable and afflicted) is on those who fear Him with godly reverence, from generation to generation *and* age to age (Luke 1:50).

Throughout this book, I'll sometimes refer to a family as a tree (the type you see in baby books). The roots of this tree bear the family names, branches extend as new generations of families are added, and fruit appears as new family members are born. Our family trees can only bear godly fruit (children who grow up with a Father's heart) when their roots are secured in the Love of our Father—Creator of us all.

> For You did form my inward parts; You did knit me together in my mother's womb. I will confess *and* praise You *for You are fearful and wonderful and* for the awful wonder of my birth! Wonderful are Your works, and that my inner self knows right well. My frame was not hidden from You when
>
> I was being formed in secret [and] intricately *and* curiously wrought [as if embroidered with various colors] in the depths of the earth [a region of darkness and mystery]. Your eyes saw my unformed substance, and in Your book all the days [of my life] were written before ever they took shape, when as yet there was none of them (Psalm 139:13-16).

Even though we sometimes wander away from our Creator and Father, He wants all of His children to come back to Him through His Son, Jesus. Won't you give Him your life? The life He so dearly paid for on the cross?

> For God so greatly loved and dearly prized the world that He [even] gave up His only begotten (unique) Son, so that whoever believes in (trusts in, clings to, relies on) Him shall not perish (come to destruction, be lost) but have eternal (everlasting) life.
>
> God did not send the Son into the world in order to judge (to reject, to condemn, to pass sentence on) the world, but that the world might find salvation and be made safe and sound through Him (John 3:16-17).

Will you take a moment to believe in the eternal life Father offers you, and welcome His Son Jesus into your heart? I promise, you will never be the same!

> For with the heart a person believes (adheres to, trusts in, and relies on Christ) and so is justified (declared righteous, acceptable to God), and with the mouth he confesses (declares openly and speaks out freely his faith) and confirms [his] salvation (Romans 10:10).

The Father's Heart: Empowering Parents in Marriage

Establishing the Kingdom of God in the home is our priority as parents because every issue in life whether good or bad flows out of the family. But what is an authentic family? Let's answer that by looking at the first family designed by our Father:

> The Lord God said, It is not good (sufficient, satisfactory) that the man should be alone; I will make him a helper (suitable, adapted, complementary) for him. And out of the ground the Lord God formed every [wild] beast and living creature of the field and every bird of the air and brought them to Adam to see what he would call them;

> and whatever Adam called every living creature, that was its name. And Adam gave names to all the livestock and to the birds of the air and to every [wild] beast of the field; but for Adam there was not found a helper meet (suitable, adapted, complementary) for him.
>
> And the Lord God caused a deep sleep to fall upon Adam; and while he slept, He took one of his ribs or a part of his side and closed up the [place with] flesh. And the rib or part of his side which the Lord God had taken from the man He built up and made into a woman, and He brought her to the man.
>
> Then Adam said, This [creature] is now bone of my bones and flesh of my flesh; she shall be called Woman, because she was taken out of a man. Therefore a man shall leave his father and his mother and shall become united and cleave to his wife, and they shall become one flesh. And the man and his wife were both naked and were not embarrassed or ashamed in each other's presence (Genesis 2:18-25).
>
> They are no longer two, but one flesh. What therefore God has joined together, let not man put asunder (separate). They said to Him, Why then did Moses command [us] to give a certificate of divorce and thus to dismiss and repudiate a wife? He said to them, Because of the hardness (stubbornness and perversity) of your hearts Moses permitted you to dismiss and repudiate and divorce your wives; but from the beginning it has not been so [ordained] (Matthew 19:6-8; see also Deuteronomy 24:1-4).

Divorce has never been God's intention for our families. When we break our marriage covenant, it allows easy access to the intruder—the enemy, the adversary who does not want you to succeed. Divorce creates roots of bitterness, rejection, and daddy/mommy issues in children, planting fear in their hearts as they wonder what will happen to them if their single parent abandons them, too. I call that fear "the spirit of abandonment," which no child should have to experience.

The fear of abandonment is just one result of divorce, which can sometimes appear to be child abuse because too many injustices (poverty, loneliness, distrust, poor grades, depression and others) occur when selfishness (often the root cause of divorce) spreads its evil tentacles. Selfishness is "the exclusive regard of a person to his own happiness; or that supreme self-love or self-preference, which leads a person in his actions to direct his purposes to the advancement of his own interest, power or happiness, without regarding the interest of others."[5]

What happens to children who are raised by selfish parents—parents who spend their time, money, and efforts advancing their own happiness? They become selfish parents, too, unless God sovereignly intervenes.

Selfishness, in its worst or unqualified sense, is the very essence of human depravity; it stands in direct opposition to benevolence, which is the essence of the divine character. As God is love, so man in his natural state is selfish:

> And this you do with double guilt; you cover the altar of the Lord with tears [shed by your unoffending wives, divorced by you that you might take heathen wives], and with [your own] weeping and crying out because the Lord does not regard your offering any more or accept it with favor at your hand.
>
> Yet you ask, Why does He reject it? Because the Lord was witness [to the covenant made at your marriage] between you and the wife of your youth, against whom you have dealt treacher-

> ously and to whom you were faithless. Yet she is your companion and the wife of your covenant [made by your marriage vows].
>
> And did not God make [you and your wife] one [flesh]? Did not One make you and preserve your spirit alive? And why [did God make you two] one? Because He sought a godly offspring [from your union]. Therefore take heed to yourselves, and let no one deal treacherously and be faithless to the wife of his youth.
>
> For the Lord, the God of Israel, says: I hate divorce and marital separation and him who covers his garment [his wife] with violence. Therefore keep a watch upon your spirit [that it may be controlled by My Spirit], that you deal not treacherously and faithlessly [with your marriage mate] (Malachi 2:13-16).

This is a lot to consider, I know, but these particular Scriptures tell us how Father views separation, divorce, and violence in marriage. Father is saying that He was there when we made our marriage vows; He was a witness when we as man and wife promised to stay with each other in sickness, in health, in wealth, in sacrificing to build a business, and through all of the ups and downs in life. And He wants us to be there for each other, too.

Knowing this, when Dez and I got married in 1979, we wrote our marriage vows using affirmations from our hearts. Instead of "till death do us part," we said, "as long as we both shall live to love" simply because we both believe in eternal life. In our covenant marriage, we live to love not to death. That has become a seal of our marriage, a pillar, and it has stayed with me through all times we disagree and even argue about our needs and wants.

We have to guard our hearts with diligence because the issues of life can cause us to speak faithlessly and treacherously to our spouses. This hardness of heart is often the spark that fuels a dysfunctional family.

When relationships start to deteriorate, the question of "how did this happen?" lingers in our minds. The answer is that it started a long time ago in the little things that each other said or didn't say. It went unnoticed until life in the home got, as they say, "real bad." If you're not listening, hearing, or talking to your spouse, then who are you listening, hearing, or talking to? Quite often, the answer is the enemy (in one form or another), the one who seeks to destroy your family—and often succeeds. Attacks on marriage and the family in the spiritual arena are rampant; however, as you read through these pages, we'll see that we've been given the tools from Father to overcome everything in life. It's up to us to use them.

This book is not written to concentrate on divorce; we all know the statistics, and they are bleak—both in and outside of the body of Christ. I want to focus on marriage as a covenant and how that covenant operates as part of the foundation that we build upon in raising HIS PRECIOUS CARGO.

Let's start!

Wholeness Is His Design

I used to hear people say in reference to marriage, "Two halves make a whole." Now, when did God ever make half of a person? We're all made in the likeness and image of a loving Creator, Almighty God, so we should be advancing toward Him with us (beings of light) who are complete in Him.

This means that before getting married, you need to be a whole human being (knowing who you are in Him). In other words, you are an individual before you get married;

marriage should then enhance who you already are. You don't get married so that the other person completes you; there is only One completer and His name is Christ Jesus, Yeshua our Messiah.

Neither husband nor wife can complete each other in that sense. That also means you don't get married for money, houses, emotional stability, loneliness, missing mommies, absent daddies, or a host of other maladies. Why?

Because

> houses and riches are the inheritance from fathers, but a wise, understanding, and prudent wife is from the Lord (Proverbs 19:14).

And

> he who finds a (true) wife finds a good thing and obtains favor from the Lord (Proverbs 18:22).

And

> a capable, intelligent, and virtuous woman—who is he who can find her? She is far more precious than jewels and her value is far above rubies or pearls (Proverbs 31:10).

Ladies, our Creator does not say she who finds a husband does He? No! He says *he who finds a wife*. Our place is to be very prayerful and discerning to make sure he who finds us is the real deal straight from Father; that means not every man who finds us is the real deal. Check for his fruit, and watch!

> Beware of false prophets, who come to you dressed as sheep, but inside they are devouring wolves. You will fully recognize them by their fruits. Do people pick grapes from thorns, or figs from thistles? Even so, every healthy (sound)

> tree bears good fruit [worthy of admiration], but the sickly (decaying, worthless) tree bears bad (worthless) fruit. A good (healthy) tree cannot bear bad (worthless) fruit, nor can a bad (diseased) tree bear excellent fruit [worthy of admiration]. Every tree that does not bear good fruit is cut down and cast into the fire. Therefore, you will fully know them by their fruits (Matthew 7:15-20).

Our minds might tell us that we're whole, but we still might bring baggage into our marriages, dirty laundry that counseling did not detect or rid us of, such as the hurts of broken relationships that lead to a spirit of rejection in our heart. I call this spirit the "not-good-enough spirit." Only the intimacy of Father through our Lord will annihilate it. Only He can validate you like you need to be validated. No one heals like the Father—no one.

Even if we have no such rejection hanging over our soul, we should all want to know and be intimately acquainted with Father in all His ways before we get married because "in Him we live and move and have our being ... for we are also His offspring" (Acts 17:28).

Before I got married, I really didn't trust men, and I know it was because of the way my parents' marriage ended after thirteen years. Yet, I still planned to marry Dez, and I even took on the task of planning a beautiful wedding for us that centered on the vows, the music, the whole ceremony. But just two weeks before the wedding, I told Dez that he had to promise me two things: The first being that he could not run around on me (commit adultery), and the second was that he could not be stingy concerning money. I told him, "If you think you're going to break the first promise, then maybe we shouldn't get married."

Not only that, I also said, "If you do break it, I'll make your life miserable by never getting married again and keeping all my military privileges. And if we have children, I'll fight for custody so that you'll have to pay child support every month, and that means you won't have enough money to ever get married again!"

Of course, these promises were a result of the hurt I still felt toward my earthly dad for breaking up our family. I made a vow for handling this potential betrayal; I had a plan, and it was not from the Lord!

Dez said, "Okay."

And with that, the wedding was on!

I asked him later, "Why did you say okay?"

"I knew that you always had a good heart," he said. "Naive, but good."

Did Dez and I come to our marriage being whole? No! We both had "daddy issues"; therefore, Father had to heal us through and through as we humbled ourselves and submitted to His Spirit, whom we call Holy Spirit.

> Humble yourselves [feeling very insignificant] in the presence of the Lord, and He will exalt you [He will lift you up and make your lives significant] (James 4:10).

Dez and I humbled ourselves when we entered into God's covenant of marriage, a legally binding contract in the spiritual and natural realms, with Father as our witness. One meaning of covenant means "literally a coming together; a meeting or agreement of minds."[6] The idea of a covenant is so dear to our Father. Think of all the covenants in the Bible made by God to Israel, by men to other men, and by men to the wives of their youth.

The best covenant of all, though, is the Blood covenant by our Lord and Savior Jesus— Yeshua, our Messiah—made to each of us. From Genesis to Revelation, we can read about the immeasurable grace He has given us through His suffering, dying, and resurrection. Like all of His promises, His Blood covenant is a promise He will never forsake.

If Almighty God always keeps His covenant promises to us, how much more should we who are in His Kingdom? He loves us no matter how many faults we have because He looks at us through Christ Jesus our Messiah. Shouldn't we do the same for our not-so-perfect spouses? Why? Because none of us are perfect, no not one.

Dez and I have been married for thirty-three years as of October 2012. Our marriage covenant has lasted, largely, because we both took the words *divorce* and *separation* out of our vocabulary before we got married. We understood what we were getting into, at least half of it, and we agreed to embark on an adventure into the other half. The other reason our covenant has endured is that from the beginning, both of us loved the Lord and allowed Holy Spirit to work out a lot of things in us—and it was not easy.

You, also have to submit to God and be committed to your spouse through the Holy Spirit. This means allowing Him to help you subdue your flesh, your tongue, and all the other things that cause destruction in the home and, instead, come into agreement with love and a focus on Him. As we entered marriage, Dez and I agreed immediately on how to handle some issues, such as raising children, me having a career, helping our mothers, budgeting, and fully operating as one unit in everything we did. To accomplish this, we had to allow Holy Spirit to work Himself out in us.

> I appeal to you therefore, brethren, *and* beg of you in view of [all] the mercies of God, to make a decisive dedication of your bodies [presenting all

> your members and faculties] as a living sacrifice, holy (devoted, consecrated) and well pleasing to God, which is your reasonable (rational, intelligent) service *and* spiritual worship.
>
> Do not be conformed to this world (this age), [fashioned after and adapted to its external, superficial customs], but be transformed (changed) by the [entire] renewal of your mind [by its new ideals and its new attitude], so that you may prove [for yourselves] what is the good and acceptable and perfect will of God, *even* the thing which is good and acceptable and perfect [in His sight for you] (Romans 12:1-2 AMP).

Alongside the Holy Spirit's guidance and work in us, I cannot overemphasize the importance of communication in marriage. I can remember when I would be caught up working on different things in the house and Holy Spirit would say in that still small voice, *go and talk with your husband*. He doesn't skip a beat, He knows all and will tell you (if you are constantly moving toward Him) the little things to make your marriage secure in Him. That, in itself, reaps such a harvest because when you communicate with your spouse, you don't lean toward the lies, the answers from the intruder to the questions floating around in your head and heart. How often I thought Dez was thinking or doing something, only to find out after we talked that was not the case.

The Father Has a Heart for Single Parents

Yes, as a single parent you can still raise godly children whose heart is after God—because His heart is always after you. Don't try to be both parents because you can't. Father made you a mother or father, but not both. You were created for the role you are in, so don't try to be supermom or superdad. Give your children to Him, and He will direct you to His favor (more about that in chapter four). He will also direct you to the people, and to the plans He has for them. Remember, God sets the solitary in families (Psalm 68:6), and so the person you need to lean on and depend on while being a single parent is also Holy Spirit.

If you would like to learn more about the challenges and victories of single-parenting, please read *Growing Up With a Single Parent: What Hurts, What Helps* by Sara McLanahan and Gary Sandefur. Keep in mind, however, that even with the authors' experience and wisdom, Holy Spirit has power that man does not, and that makes all the difference in the world when overcoming the hurts of growing up with a single parent.

God Longs to Bless the Family

The promise to bless a thousand generations was first given to Abraham, and it's still coming to fruition. We have to embrace the blessings that Father has for the family unit because He longs to bless us with His promises, just like He promised to bless Abraham's family. But before God could bless him, Abraham had to prove that God could trust him. Father told us that He did trust Abraham when He said of him:

> I have known (chosen, acknowledged) him [as My own], **so that he may teach and command** his children and the sons of his house after him to keep the way of the Lord and to do what is just and righteous, so that the Lord may bring Abraham what He has promised him (Genesis 18:19, emphasis mine).

One of the meanings for "command" is the Hebrew word *tsavah*, which basically means to constitute, to charge, to establish a rule, obligation, or duty.[7] It can also mean to direct and instruct, as in a father's instruction and a mother's teaching in Proverbs 1:8 and 4:1.

Dez and I chose to just do it (our marriage and our parenting) God's way by following His teaching and commands and leading. When we did, there was no stopping what we could accomplish as a couple. Did we ever make mistakes? We most certainly did. We assessed our mistake; went back in prayer to listen to God; waited to hear Him correctly because He is never, never wrong; then we changed our ways and moved forward.(Ladies, if you have a trust issue with men—be it earthly fathers or your spouse—that lack of trust will affect how much you trust Father God. You have to trust Father to obey Him, so pray to Father for healing in that area.)

Dez and I knew that we had to rid our marriage from the junk, trip-ups, oops! and the what just happened? We call these baggage items the "bait of the enemy" because that's what these distractions are intended to catch—us, off guard. We needed all the strategy we could get from Holy Spirit to throw away our dirty laundry, and fill that empty space with Him—and we got it.

Since Dez and I were both raised without fathers that added to our zeal for doing whatever we needed to do to make sure our marriage lasts forever. Thankfully, both sets of grandparents on our mothers' sides were never divorced; they remained joyously in love, and their example encouraged us to do likewise.

When times get rough, though, and our love is tested, I remain in prayer and remember our covenant before Father through a thirty-three year old photograph. Our wedding photographer took a picture (double exposure) of me and

Dez repeating our marriage vows in front of a stained glass window with an image of the Lord holding His hands up to heaven in blessing.

That picture has gotten me through times when I felt overwhelmed—times when we were packing to move again, when Dez was in military class in another state, when our sons were getting on my first and last nerve, and when Dez and I exchanged words over stupid stuff. After my prayer time, during each of these events, I would look at that picture.

Almost thirty-three years of picture-viewing has passed, and I ask myself, Would I do this marriage thing all over again? I look at my husband and my sons, and I answer a resounding YES! You can make it through the difficult times, too. Just allow the Lord to make the two of you truly one unit, a force to be reckoned with. And remember, one of you can put a thousand to flight but the two of you together can put ten thousand to flight. Who are you putting to flight? The intruders. You have this power because the Greatest One lives in you!

Shalom; the peace of God be over your marriage.

FATHER, in the name of Jesus, I thank You for every married couple whose eyes are upon these words, which You by Your Spirit have imparted to me to write.

I thank You for wisdom and understanding.

I thank You that couples' eyes will be opened and they will be given ears to hear.

I thank You for clear communication with an understanding of what these couples are saying, or trying to say from the heart to each other.

I thank You that they will only hear Your voice, and another voice they will not hear nor follow.

I thank You for humbleness of heart at all times.

I thank You Lord God for honesty.

I thank You that the marriage bed stays pure and will not be shared outside the confines of marriage (Hebrews 13:4).

I thank You that couples are transformed in the love they have for each other.

I pray that the love, adoration, and respect they have for each other grows, that the husband will love his wife according to Ephesians 5:21-33, that unity will prevail in every area of their lives, and that they will continue to grow together to become a force that says they can accomplish all things through Christ who strengthens them. We know greater is He who is in us than he who is in the world.

I thank You that these couples are proactive in their marriages, and I declare and decree that no weapon formed against them will be able to prosper—in Jesus' name—and that the peace of the Lord will prevail over and in their household every day before the sun sets.

For all the marriages that have been fruitful in You, I thank You that they are examples to Your great love through our Lord and Savior Christ Jesus, Amen.

It is easier to build strong children
than to repair broken men.

~ Frederick Douglas,
American social reformer, orator,
writer, and statesman

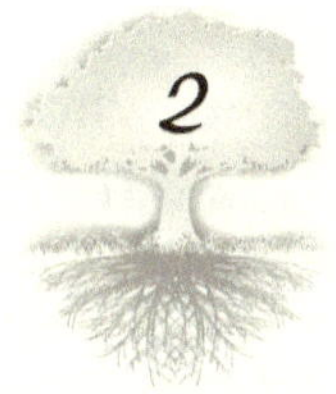

2

Preparing Fertile Soil (Praying for Your Children)

> Lord, You must now teach us to pray, just as also John taught his disciples.
>
> ~ Luke 11:1 PNT

It would be robbery if I gave you a bunch of prayers and said, "Just pray these over your children." It's Father's will that I, instead, teach you how to pray for your children through your relationship with Father through His Son Christ Jesus. No matter how simple you think your prayers are, He will receive them if they are from your heart.

> Confess to one another therefore your faults (your slips, your false steps, your offenses, your sins) and pray [also] for one another, that you may be healed *and* restored [to a spiritual tone of mind and heart]. The earnest (heartfelt, continued) prayer of a righteous man makes tremendous power available [dynamic in its working] (James 5:16).

I am an early riser, and when our sons were young, I woke up every day at least an hour or two before waking everyone else. This enabled me to have quiet time with Father before getting us all ready for the day. Whatever Holy Spirit led me to do that morning, that's what I did. Sometimes I wrote prayers in my journal or meditated on the Word or sang hymns, and other songs that I would hear as I meditated. Other times, I sat quietly so I could hear His voice.

Here is a prayer that I wrote in one of my prayer journals dated 8 February 2000:

> Dear Father in Heaven, make yourself known personally to our sons. Oh that they may know You. Direct our sons, strengthen our household. Keep the groundwork of the fear of the Lord, Your integrity, prosperity, and shalom of the whole man for this entire family in Jesus.

When I look at my journals, I see how I so prayed for and then thanked Him for giving God-like character to our sons, along with His virtues, grace, and mercy.

You can pray for your children, too. Open your Bible and go through the promises in the Word concerning your children. Read the stories in the Old Testament, and see if Holy Spirit has something to say to you concerning your children. Read through the New Testament, and ask Father that everything *He* promises be granted to your sons and daughters. Start a conversation with Him about your children's needs and desires, remembering that each child is different, unique, and blessed of the Lord.

When I thank Him in my heart for being Who He is and what He has already done, my heart becomes intertwined with His, and I find myself effortlessly praying just what was on His heart all along. It's so important to know that prayer starts with praise.

The Blessedness of Giving Praise and Thanksgiving

Psalm 100 tells us to enter His gates with thanksgiving in our hearts and enter His courts with praise. I love a sweatless victory; and when I have the right heart attitude about who He is and what He has done for me, my whole person rejoices! So before you start praying, prepare your heart to enter into fellowship with Him:

- Thank Him for His greatness
- Ask Father to forgive you of any sin you have committed (Matthew 6)
- Forgive everyone who has offended you
- Repent (change your mind and ways from the way you used to think to how God wants you to think)
- Meditate on the Word before Him

To meditate on His Word means allowing Holy Spirit to come in and enlighten, (make clear, expound, expand, insight, understanding, and give a meaning to a verse which you have not realized before). For instance, allow the Spirit of the Lord to choose a verse from a chapter you are reading, such as Luke 11:1: "teach us to pray, just as also John taught his disciples."

Start a conversation with yourself and Holy Spirit about the Word. Ask Holy Spirit about any questions or answers you're not sure about, like "What did it mean to the disciples to pray?" To answer questions about meanings of words, invest in a good Bible Concordance and Bible Dictionary because they will give you the meanings of words based on the language and time in which the Bible was written.

We forget that the original language of the Bible was not English; the Old Testament was written in Hebrew/Aramaic. And the New Testament was written by our brothers, the Jewish apostles, in the Greek language. A word in the Bible takes on a very different meaning in these languages. Knowing these meanings will help you discern what Holy Spirit meant when He breathed on men and inspired them to write.

So, if you are reading Luke 11:1 and want to know more about what the disciples meant when they said, "teach us to pray," look up "pray" in your concordance and note Strong's number for the word "pray" as used in Luke 11:1. This reference number is "4336" and the Greek word is *proseúxomai.* Then look up 4336 in a Strong's Dictionary to get its definition—to supplicate (we'll see more definitions of prayer below).

To get a broader perspective of the meaning of *proseúxomai,* read other verses that use the same Greek word. This will give you a well-rounded feel for how this particular word for "pray" is used in biblical times.

This process of finding word meanings is a dialogue with God and language, and I love it! But don't get too involved in the quantity of verses you read. Our Father is very patient and we should be, too, as we meditate on His Word. Meditate and wait on the Lord to answer you concerning what you did or did not understand.

Don't forget to thank Him for spending time with you. Father loves it when we acknowledge and honor Him by thanking Him for everything He does for us.

When your heart is ready, you can begin your prayer time with God.

What is Prayer?

What does it mean to enter into prayer with our Father? Let's look into the meaning of "pray" and "prayer" using a variety of word tools. The *Webster's 1828 American Dictionary of the English Language* helps us understand these words:

Pray

To ask with earnestness, zeal, as for a favor, for something desirable, to entreat, and to supplicate. "Pray for them who despitefully use you and persecute you" (Matthew 5).

To petition; to ask, as for a favor; as in application to a legislative body.

In worship, to address the Supreme Being with solemnity and reverence, with adoration, confession of sins, supplication for mercy, and thanksgiving for blessings received (Matthew 6).

I pray, that is, I pray you tell me, or let me know, is a common mode of introducing a question.[1]

Prayer

In a general sense, the act of asking for a favor, and particularly with earnestness.

In worship, a solemn address to the Supreme Being, consisting of adoration, or an expression of our sense of God's glorious perfections, confession of our sins, supplication for mercy and forgiveness, intercession for blessings on others, and thanksgiv-

> ing, or an expression of gratitude to God for His mercies and benefits.
>
> A prayer however may consist of a single petition, and it may be extemporaneous, written or printed. A formula of church service, or of worship, public or private. Practice of supplication.[2]

Adding to the above definitions, "pray" and "prayer" in *The New Strong's Expanded Dictionary of Bible Words* can have different meanings according to the context of the Scripture in which it is used. For example, Joseph's brothers were very afraid of what Joseph might do to them after their father had passed. They said to Joseph, "I pray you now…" (Genesis 50:17). This word for "pray" in the Hebrew is *ânnâ,* which means, "Oh now, I ask you!"[3]

We also read about Jesus telling us to pray for those that persecute us (Matthew 5:44). Here, the word "pray" is *proseuchomai* in the Greek (as we read earlier in Luke 11:1), which means to supplicate or to pray. [4]

To get a general idea of what prayer can do for you, consider these action words associated with "pray" and "prayer."

> Pray
>
> To be weak; to implore; to impinge; to intercede; to ask; to ponder, muse aloud; to beg, petition, ask; to interrogate; to request; to wish for; to pray; to call, invite; to supplicate, pray. Oh now, I ask you!;
>
> Prayer
>
> To be weak; intercede in prayer; to ponder, muse aloud; uttered contemplation; petition, request;

> intercession; wish, petition; prayer; prayer chapel; and to supplicate, pray. Prayer, for me, is the weakening, the imploring, the interceding, the petitioning, the leaning of my whole self on my Father through Jesus, recognizing that He is Creator and I'm the created.

When I pray, I realize He has the answers to everything in life, Christ in me is the Hope of glory because I can do all things though Christ who strengthens me, I have a Father who loves me and knows what I need because He alone made me a human, a being of Life.

Prayer: What a Privilege and an Honor!

Now that we understand what prayer is, when and how do we pray? When I feel Holy Spirit leading me to pray for the fruitfulness of my sons, for example, I might turn to Psalm 1:3 and pray: "Lord, I thank You that our sons are 'like trees firmly planted (and tended) by the streams of water, ready to bring forth its fruit in its season; its leaf also shall not fade or wither; and everything he does shall prosper (and come to maturity)."

Did you notice I thanked Him for the promise first because I intend to listen for the instructions from Him on how to raise our sons up to become that fruitful tree. In essence, prayer changes people and situations; need I say more?

Let's take a look at Psalm 128, verses 3-4 in two versions to meditate on in prayer for your children. I chose this passage because I love it; it really hits a homerun on how Father sees our children. Please allow Holy Spirit to speak to your heart as you read and ponder them.

> Your wife will be like a fruitful vine within your house; your children will be like olive shoots around your table. Yes, this will be the blessing for the man who fears the Lord (NIV).

> Your wife will bear children as a vine bears grapes, your household lush as a vineyard, the children around your table as fresh and promising as young olive shoots. Stand in awe of God's Yes. Oh, how he blesses the one who fears God! (MSG).

To really understand the meaning of these verses and how they apply to your children, it is helpful to understand that olive trees are some of the oldest living trees in our world with a life span that extends beyond hundreds of years. They are often pictured with baby olive shoots as tender plants surrounding the adult trees.

Our children (whether biological or spiritual) are said to be like olive shoots; we push them forth sending them out, full of vigor, virtue, and vitality. They draw from the parent tree (God-fearing parents) everything they need for life and, therefore, they are able to continue in life, bearing the fruit of the Father. This is the blessing of the Lord—the posterity of the family line living in God's will, on purpose, as He created us to be (Genesis 1).

That blessing is exactly what this book is about—preparing the soil (the foundation) for the seed to germinate and the tree to break forth bearing much fruit. There is a fruitful tree inside of every seed. The question is, are we as parents going to give that seed what is needed to become a fruitful tree?

We can help to grow our seeds into phenomenal fruit-bearers through the power of prayer. Below are some Scriptures that I meditate on and turn into prayers depending on the situation in my life or my children's lives. This list is not exhaustive. As you begin to hear Holy Spirit more and more and recognize His voice, He will direct you to Scriptures tailor-made for your child. Do not forget to study the Word with your tools (Bible Dictionary and Concordance) and stay open to the leading of Holy Spirit as you meditate and pray.

Here are some of my favorite verses to meditate on regarding specific needs in my family over the years. I've also included a couple of sample prayers for others and for yourself:

Conception

> May ADONAI increase your numbers, both yours and those of your children. May you be blessed by ADONAI, the maker of heaven and earth. Heaven belongs to ADONAI, but the earth he has given to humankind (Psalm 115:14-16 CJB).

- Genesis 1:28-29
- Genesis 16:15 (whole chapter)
- Genesis 30:22
- Deuteronomy 7:14
- Deuteronomy 28:4

Difficult Pregnancies

- Psalm 89:1-5
- Psalm 91 (entire chapter)
- Psalm 121 (entire chapter)
- Samuel 1:12-27
- Psalm 127:3
- Psalm 113:9
- Luke 1:5-20

Newborns

- Psalm 8:1-9
- Psalm 22:9-10
- Psalm 22:30-31
- Psalm 27:10 (AMP)
- Psalm 78:1-5
- Psalm 139:13-16

Posterity of Family Line

- I Chronicles 16:15
- Psalm 22:34
- Psalm 33:11
- Psalm 45:17
- Psalm 61:6-8
- Psalm 79:13
- Psalm 89:1
- Psalm 90:1
- Psalm 102:12
- Psalm 102:28
- Psalm 112:1-3
- Psalm 119:90
- Psalm 145:4
- Isaiah 41:4
- Isaiah 45:8
- 2 Timothy 2:10

Salvation

- Isaiah 54:13

Heart Matters: Integrity and Character

Father, I ask for an understanding mind and a hearing heart to discern between good and evil. Thank you Father for a wise, discerning heart for Dezmond, Dominick, Joshua and Jacob in the name of Jesus, Amen.

- I Kings 2:9
- Proverbs 2:2; 2:10
- Proverbs 3:1-35
- Proverbs chapter 4
- Proverbs 8:5
- Proverbs 14:14; 30-33
- Proverbs 15:13, 28
- Proverbs 16:9, 21
- Proverbs 17:16
- Proverbs 18:15
- Proverbs 20:5
- Proverbs 22:11
- Proverbs 23:7, 12, 15, 17
- Proverbs 25:3

There are so many Scriptures you can use for prayer for your children, so please allow Holy Spirit to lead you into all truth concerning them. Every prayer can be as unique as each child because Holy Spirit will show you what to pray for each child.

Communicating the Heart of Father

Not only did I keep prayer journals while my sons were growing up; when they were away from home, I wrote letters and cards to encourage them in the Lord. Though Dezmond attended a Christian University with a spirit of excellence, he was still our son, and so we wrote, called, and shared the beauty, grace, and mercy of Father God for us all. He recently gave me all the letters and cards I sent him when he was away his freshman year in college, and they were detailed.

I remember on 9/11 of 2001, Dezmond was a freshman in college in Oklahoma. I had been up since three in the morning reading the Book of Acts and enjoying hearing from the Holy Spirit what purpose and plans He had for Dezmond's life. I started writing a letter to Dezmond and shared with him everything that I heard from Holy Spirit. He really mapped out what He had planned for my son before the foundations of the world.

Why did Holy Spirit share this with me? Because as parents, we have an obligation to declare and decree what we hear the Lord speaking to us concerning our children's purpose and destiny, which I call the Divine Calling (the thing for which they were created to do as part of their worship to God). We war (bring petitions to God concerning what He has spoken) for their divine (prophetic) calling. We don't give Him rest until He–by His Spirit–brings it to pass.

The Blessedness of the Blessing

The Lord told Moses how Aaron (the high priest) should bless the Israelites, and Dez would bless our sons the same way—laying his hands on their heads as he decreed Aaron's priestly blessing over their lives:

> The Lord bless you and watch, guard, and keep you; the Lord make His face to shine upon and enlighten you and be gracious (kind, merciful, and giving favor) to you; The Lord lift up His [approving] countenance upon you and give you peace (tranquility of heart and life continually). And they shall put My name upon the Israelites, and I will bless them (Numbers 6:22-27).

It's so important to bless our children. The word "bless" is the Hebraic word *barak,* which means to kneel, bless, and be blesssed.[5] When we are blessed, we are empowered to prosper and multiply that prosperity in every area of our lives: our calling, purpose, giving, education, vocations in life, blessings to the nations, whatever we put our hands on should be blessed.

The other word "peace" is the Hebraic word *shalowm,* which means safe, welfare, health, rest, peace, and wholeness.[6] Do you see the tremendous power in speaking these words over your children every day? You would reap such a harvest of blessings for your generational line if you prayed blessing over them.

Father God really loves and cares for His children and doesn't want any one of us to perish for lack of knowledge, so we choose to speak blessings in their lives, especially those contained in the Beatitudes (Matthew 5:1-12) because these words contain so many virtues that you want to see grow in your child. *Noah Webster's 1828 Dictionary* says the Beatitudes are

> blessedness; felicity of the highest kind; consummate bliss used of the joys of Heaven;
>
> The declaration of blessedness by our Savior to particular virtues.

I have seen first-hand the powerful results of speaking these blessings. In Port Elizabeth (Nelson Mandela Bay) South Africa, in 2004, I spoke with two other women in a particular township where the effects of racial inequality from the former apartheid remained in full force. We had another engagement to get to, so there wasn't much time for us to speak. The praise period went on for about an hour because the people lived for the joy of the Lord despite their deep poverty. I take off my hat to those in ministry there, living in similar conditions, teaching the native South Africans different ways to use their giftings and talents to prosper and be self-sustaining.

Even with so much joy, I sensed a spirit of poverty and despair, so I asked Holy Spirit, "What can I say in such a short time to bring encouragement to the people?" He gave me a strong urging to read the Beatitudes from the Amplified Bible. Our interpreter interpreted with so much drama and elaboration that every time he spoke, the crowd of about 500-750 went crazy praising God. You see, blessings give hope, and hope spurs us into trust and faith in the Lord. The faces of those native South Africans reflected a spark of hope because they recognized what Father was saying to them from His Word.

On the front cover of this book, you'll see Dez blessing Dominick. Lay hands on your children, and speak the blessing of the Lord over them so that they, too, become a blessing to others wherever Father places them.

Wisdom—The Principle Thing!

Dez and I pursued building the character of the Lord in our sons when they were very young by reading Proverbs to them. Then, when Dezmond was in middle school and Dominick in elementary school, we trained them to read and meditate on one chapter of Proverbs a day. Each chapter number corresponded to the day of the month on which they would read it. We started Jacob and Joshua on this plan when they came to live with us in 1997. Some days, we would sit and discuss what we had read, and we made sure we used Bibles they could understand.

We started this reading because we all tend to think that we have gained a lot of wisdom from life's experiences, but it's really man's wisdom. Solomon was only a child when he became king following his father's passing, and he asked the Lord for wisdom that he may rule the people fairly; he had no life experiences. He had Wisdom from on high, God's Wisdom, which gave answers to questions and problems he encountered. That is the Wisdom we should want for our children—that supernatural Wisdom—which I call "a keeper" because it keeps them out of trouble before, not after, a problem occurs.

Let me quote from Proverbs chapter one and other Scriptures so that you may understand the importance of reading and meditating on Wisdom when raising your child:

> The proverbs (truths obscurely expressed, maxims, and parables) of Solomon son of David, king of Israel: That people may know skillful and godly Wisdom and instruction, discern and comprehend the words of understanding and insight, receive instruction in wise dealing and the discipline of wise thoughtfulness, righteousness, justice, and integrity, that prudence may be

> given to the simple, and knowledge, discretion, and discernment to the youth—the wise also will hear and increase in learning, and the person of understanding will acquire skill and attain to sound counsel [so that he may be able to steer his course rightly] (Proverbs 1:1-5).

> The reverent fear and worship of the Lord is the beginning of Wisdom and skill [the preceding and the first essential, the prerequisite and the alphabet]; a good understanding, wisdom, and meaning have all those who do [the will of the Lord]. Their praise of Him endures forever (Psalm 111:10).

> My son, hear the instruction of your father; reject not nor forsake the teaching of your mother. For they are a [victor's] chaplet (garland) of grace upon your head and chains and pendants [of gold worn by kings] for your neck. My son, if sinners entice you, do not consent (Proverbs 1:8-10; see also Psalm 1:1; Ephesians 5:11).

Proverbs speak about every subject that we as parents will eventually have to discuss with our children—subjects about the reverential fear of the Lord, honoring parents, respect for human beings, the company they keep, sex, money matters, being committed in marriage (chapter 5 and more), cursing (chapter 4), how to choose a wife, and integrity in all issues of life, including conducting your business affairs. Father left nothing out when Holy Spirit breathed on Proverbs.

The book of Proverbs is loaded with Wisdom for the person who desires to live a disciplined godly lifestyle. This

Wisdom is timeless and transcends national and ethnic barriers. In March 2004, I was blessed to be one of two women speakers at a church in Port Elizabeth (Nelson Mandela Bay), South Africa. We were guests at a luncheon given in our honor the day before a Women's Conference.

They asked me about raising children, so I spoke to them about the importance of using Proverbs as a foundation for raising children in the fear and admonition of the Lord. I showed them, as I have done above, how Proverbs will help their sons and daughters navigate themselves in a godly way through all life situations. They simply loved this idea; as the years passed, the reports came in to show how they had implemented the Proverbs and raised godly children.

Equally Yoked

I was praying with my husband for our children's mates when I heard the Spirit of the Lord say to me, "Uh uh! Now turn it around, and pray that your sons would become God-fearing husbands for their wives!"

That kind of rebuke knocked the wind right out of my prayers. So I reversed my prayers and started asking God for certain attributes that our sons needed to have to help them become godly husbands. Here are some of the Scriptures I used:

- Colossians 3:5-9: Stripping off the old self
- Ephesians 4:2-3: Peace
- Colossians 3:19: Loving your wife
- Colossians 3:21: Great fathers

Other Scriptures are applicable to raising up godly daughters in marriage. I particularly love Proverbs 31 because it is so innovative for today's lady. The woman of Proverbs 31 is an entrepreneur, she's in real estate, has housekeepers, loves and communicates with her husband and children, gathers spiritual food for her family (which tells me she is a lady of godly wisdom), and trades with the nations. She does all this with a spirit of excellence. To me that is so grand!

When praying for their wives, I always prayed for a prudent woman because the Word tells us (Proverbs 19:14) that houses and riches come from fathers, but a prudent wife is from the Lord.

That word "prudent" is the word *sakal* in the Hebrew, which means act wisely, give attention to, ponder, prosper, that they may see, know, consider, and understand; insight, and intellectual comprehension.[7] Sounds like the Proverbs 31 woman to me; how about you?

I realized my sons cared about their future mates, too, when we arrived home from a family visit. It was raining. I stayed in the car praying for a niece. The guys got out, and I heard Dominick ask Dezmond, "Where are we going to find a wife just like Mom?"

"I don't know," he said. "I guess we have to pray for one."

Why pray for our children? Because prayer produces the rich soil that roots need to grow.

Our sons and daughters also need to know that they can pray to our Lord God anytime, and anywhere. So invite your children to participate in prayer when you pray. Teach them the Word and how to pray from the Word and let them be an activate participant of their own growth.

Father, I thank You for the many Scriptures You have imparted to me to share with parents.

I thank You even more for Holy Spirit speaking and showing them the purpose for which each one of their daughters and sons have been born.

Lord, I thank You for the revelation in Your Word that You have for each parent and child.

I thank You for opening up the ears to their hearts so that they may hear what the Spirit of the Lord has to say concerning their family.

Father, I thank You for testimonies concerning their children; may they realize that it is never, never, too late to pray for Your children.

Finally, all [of you] should be of one and the same mind (united in spirit), sympathizing [with one another], loving [each other] as brethren [of one household], compassionate and courteous (tenderhearted and humble).

For the eyes of the Lord are upon the righteous (those who are upright and in right standing with God), and His ears are attentive to their prayer. But the face of the Lord is against those who practice evil [to oppose them, to frustrate, and defeat them].

~ 1 Peter 3:8, 12

The child must know that he is a miracle,
that since the beginning of the world
there hasn't been,
and until the end of the world,
there will not be another child like him.

~ Pablo Casals, one of the world's
greatest musicians
and humanitarians

Naming Your Seed Wisely (Know Father's Purpose for Your Child)

"Hannibal is going to be his name! After all, he is a great warrior," said Dez.

"No," Mom said to me, "Name him after his father; after all, Henery (Dez) is such a proper English name."

Dez and my mother went back and forth about the name of our first-born. I simply loathed the name Hannibal. I couldn't tell anyone why, and my husband's name just didn't fit. I wanted our child's name to have a meaning that spoke volumes to who Father said he is.

A great emphasis is placed on names and their meanings in the Word of God. Names were given and names were changed to fit His divine purpose for people's lives. Being in His divine will is what we are created for because that is our worship to Him. There is no better place in Him then walking in the purpose and destiny for which you were created. That in itself is the blessing.

God changed the names of

- Abram (exalted father) to Abraham (father of many nations) in Genesis 17:5;
- Sarai (my princess) to Sarah (princess of nations or mother of nations) in Genesis 17:15;
- Jacob (to catch by the heel, heel catcher) to Israel (contender, fighter, God prevails, Prince of God);
- Simon (God has heard) to Peter (rock) in John 1:42.

God named Zachariah's son, John, which means "Yahweh is gracious" (Luke 1:13). He also gave Mary the name for Jesus, which in Hebrew is Yeshua and means "salvation" (Luke 1:31).

In the book of Acts, the Bible does not state that God changed Saul of Tarsus' name, and I've often pondered why Saul (later named Paul) changed his name. The name Saul means "asked for, prayed for," and Paul means "small, humble, and least." Could it be that he was remorseful in being extremely zealous, believing that those who followed Christ were wrong as he sought to jail or kill them? Or was it because of Acts 9:16: "I will show him how many things he must suffer for My name's sake"?

When I was a child, I didn't care for my name because every year, there was an abundance of Mary's in my classes. In first grade, there were three of us, so my teacher called me by my middle name, Catherine. My peers used to make fun of my name; they would say, "Her name is Mary Catherine because she is a Catholic," or "Mary, Mary, quite contrary." Because of that, I really wanted to change it.

Mother later told me an angel of the Lord had given her my name, but the idea that He wanted me to be called Mary Catherine was astonishing; who was I that He wanted me to have a special name? After reaching adulthood and studying names, I fell in love with both of my names because they reveal a part of the character of our Creator in me. Mary is Hebrew and means "spiritual awareness" and "blessed one." Catherine is Greek and means "pure and consecrated one" or "pure and esteemed one."

Listen for the Name Father Chooses

Sometimes parents choose names for their children given to them by relatives, friends, a favorite actor or actress, or by simply what sounds good, even if they make the name up. If our Creator took the time to allow Adam to name all the creatures of the earth (Genesis 2:19-20), how much more then should we take the time to ask Father, "Who is this child?" and "What is the name You have for him or her?"

When you start listening for the name that Father gives you, it will give you a clue to your child's personality and calling. When it came time for me to listen, I went to the bookstore and bought not one, but three name books. Now I had the ammo and was ready to find the suitable name for our son. Did I know we were having a son? No, I just had a feeling; I had also lost my taste for looking at baby girl's christening dresses.

I had a desire to give our son part of my husband's name, but I knew it would not be his first or middle name. The idea then came to me about using my husband's nickname, Dez, as a foundation for his first name. Dezmond Doron Ard'is was born Saturday, December 4, and his brother Dominick Jabari Ard'is arrived on Sunday August 23, almost five years later.

Two sons, same parents, same foundation, but cut very differently; yet each child has the characteristics and personalities that match the blueprints of their names. I'm going to dissect their names so that you may understand this principle, and apply it to analyzing or choosing names of your own children. I've also listed at the end of this chapter two books for researching the meanings of names.

I started my own inquiry by using these name books and biblically-based dictionaries to find the origin, spiritual meaning, and sometimes Bible verses that relate to that particular name. I wrote down descriptive words, such as "gift" or "protector" and looked up each word in *Noah Webster's 1828 Dictionary* and *The New Strong's Expanded Dictionary of Bible Words*).

Then I found Bible verses, which I felt Holy Spirit led me to regarding the name. I meditated on those verses to see if they were a right fit for my child. As you pray concerning the name of your child, Holy Spirit will lead you to Scripture, too.

The definitions listed are compiled from one or more of the resources mentioned above. Let me start the dissection with the name of my first son, Dezmond Doron Ard'is.

Dezmond: (Irish)

Gracious protector, youthful, and refreshing.

Gracious: favorable, kind, friendly, benevolent, merciful, disposed to forgive offenses, and impart unmerited blessings.

> You are a God ready to pardon, gracious and merciful, slow to anger, and of great steadfast love; and You did not forsake them (Nehemiah 9:17).

Protector: One that defends or shields from injury; evil or oppression; a defender; or a guardian. The king or sovereign is, or ought to be, the protector of the nation; the husband is the protector of his wife, and the father of his children.

Youthful: Fresh, and vigorous, as in youth.

> You must steadily flee youthful desires, and you must habitually pursue righteousness, faith, love, peace, with those who call upon the name of the Lord out of clean hearts (2 Timothy 2:22 PNT).

Refreshing: Cooling, invigorating, reviving, and re-animating.

Doron: (Hebrew)

Gift from God, wise one, favored one, and peaceful dweller.

Gift: to endow with any power of faculty, the act of giving or conferring a reward.

Wise: to understand, discern; intelligent and skillful. Properly having knowledge, the power of discerning and judging correctly, or of discriminating between what is true and what is false, between what is fit and proper, and what is improper.

> There shall be stability in your times, an abundance of salvation, wisdom, and knowledge; the reverent fear *and* worship of the Lord is your treasure *and* His (Isaiah 33:6).

Favored: Graciousness with countenance, supplied with advantages, kindness.

Peaceful: The word for "peace" in the Hebrew is the word *shalom,* which is actually spelled *shalowm,* which means safe, well, health, make complete. Peaceful would essentially mean "full of safety, wellness, health and wholeness." And the one who is our peace is Jehovah Shalom—our Father, our Lord.

Dweller: An inhabitant, a resident of some continuance in a place.

Ard'is: (French)

Diligent one

Diligent: *Yatab, yaw-tab'* in the Hebrew;

(1) Yatab does not mean to amend or improve your ways, but rather to make one's course line up with that which is pleasing to God and that which is well-pleasing in His sight.

(2) *Yatab*, as a verb, means "to be good, do well, be glad, please, do good to go well, be pleasing, be delighted, be happy."

> Whatever may be your task, work at it heartily (from the soul), as [something done] for the Lord and not for men (Colossians 3:23).

> Do you see a man diligent and skillful in his business? He will stand before kings; he will not stand before obscure men (Proverbs 22:29).

One: The word one, *nephesh* (in the Hebrew) means soul; life; person; heart. The basic meaning comes from its verbal form, *naphash*, which refers to the essence of life, the act of breathing, taking breath (Genesis 2:7). The best biblical definition is found in Psalm 103:1, where *nephesh* is defined as "all that is within" a person: "Bless the Lord, O my soul: and all that is within me, bless His holy name."

I was curious about the name Hannibal, so I looked it up and found out it means "Baal has favored."

Baal is a pagan god. No wonder I hated that name; in fact, it grieved my spirit. I'm so glad I felt and followed the nudge of Holy Spirit in that discussion. If we had named him Hannibal, I would have been so distressed upon learning the meaning that I would have changed his name.

Our baby son, Dominick Jabari, came into the world as a lively living stone (1 Peter 2:5), screaming, and letting us know, "I'm here make room for me!" His name thoroughly describes who he is.

Dominick: (Latin)

Belonging to the Lord, faithful disciple, victorious spirit, born on Sunday (and he was born on Sunday. God has a sense of humor!).

Belonging: pertaining; appertaining; being the property of; being a quality of; being appendant to; being a native of, or having a legal or permanent settlement in.

Faithful: to be trustworthy and reliable.

Disciple: to become a student, instructed one.

> Your word is a lamp for my foot and light on my path (Psalm 119:105 CJB).
>
> I take your instruction as a permanent heritage, because it is the joy of my heart (Psalm 119:111 CJB).

> And this is the will of Him Who sent Me, that I should not lose any of all that He has given Me, but that I should give new life and raise (them all) up at the last day (John 6:39).

> He who walks and lives uprightly and blamelessly, who works rightness and justice and speaks and thinks the truth in his heart, he who does not slander with his tongue, nor does evil to his friend, nor takes up a reproach against his neighbor; in whose eyes a vile person is despised, but he who honors those who fear the Lord (who revere and worship Him); who swears to his own hurt and does not change; [he who] does not put out his money for interest [to one of his own people] and who will not take a bribe against the innocent. He who does these things shall never be moved (Psalm 15:2-5).

Victorious: conquering, overcoming, and triumphant.

> But thanks be to God, who gives us the victory through our Lord Yeshua the Messiah!" (I Corinthians 15:57 CJB).

> But thanks be to God, who in the Messiah constantly leads us in a triumphal procession and through us spreads everywhere the fragrance of what it means to know Him!" (2 Corinthians 2:14 CJB).

> Because everything which has God as its Father overcomes the world. And this is what victoriously overcomes the world: our trust." (I John 5:4 CJB).

Jabari: (Swahili)

Fearless, brave, and rejoicing one.

Fearless: free from fear, bold, courageous, intrepid, and undaunted.

Courageous: strong, strength, mighty, to be alert, strengthen, courage, speed, confirm, established, fortify, steadfastly minded, obstinate, prevailed, increase.

Brave: courageous, bold, daring, intrepid, fearless of danger, as a brave warrior. It usually unites the sense of courage with the generosity and dignity of mind, qualities often united, excellent, noble, and dignified. (In modern usage, the word brave has nearly lost these meanings and applications.)

Rejoice: to delight, boast, or glory in.

> We will boast in our God all day and give thanks to your name forever (Psalm 44:9 CJB).

Rejoice: To experience joy and gladness in a high degree.

> Then he said to them, "Go, eat rich food, drink sweet drinks, and send portions to those who can't provide for themselves; for today is consecrated to our Lord. Don't be sad, because the joy of ADONAI IS YOUR STRENGTH" (Nehemiah 8:10 CJB)

> I have no greater joy than this, when I hear that my children are walking in the truth (3 John 4 PNT).

> Now to the One Who is able to keep you without stumbling and to stand before His glory blameless in extreme joy, to the only God, our Savior

> through our Lord Jesus Messiah, be glory, majesty, strength, and power before every age, both now and forever, amen (Jude 24-25 PNT).

Decreeing the Word in a Name

The meaning of your children's name can be used strategically as a prayer point for them, especially in establishing virtue. I have prayed,

> I thank You Father for making Dominick one who rejoices in You no matter what situation he finds himself in, that he would find that in acknowledging You first as Maker and Creator of all people and things that he can accomplish all things in Christ Jesus. Let his heart be filled with the joy of the Lord every morning he wakes up, fill his heart Father with a fresh psalm, song, and hymn from You so that he will delight, boast and glory in Your name all the days of his life.

Each one of our children's names (Dezmond and Dominick) has a virtue or some virtues attributed to our Father, Yeshua (Messiah Jesus), and Holy Spirit, and I pray often that Father will increase these virtues (those above and others) in them.

Since each name of our Father denotes a part of His attributes and His character, and since we are created in the likeness and image of our Father, shouldn't the names we give them signify character, virtue, and purpose? Yes, because when names are chosen with the nudge of Holy Spirit, they are a powerful tool in the nurturing and training up of a child.

A Name: Blessing or Cursing—You Choose

The Word of God tells us that the tongue has power over life and death (Proverbs 18:21). You will call the name that you give your child many times every single day. You will be speaking the meaning of that name into your child, it will either be a blessing or a curse, life or death—you choose.

In 1 Samuel 25:25, there was a guy whose name was Nabel. Nabel is a "boar," which means rude in manners, foolish, and illiterate. This was clearly how he acted, and he died being a fool.

Saul (1 Samuel 8:19-22, 12:12-13) became the king that the people asked for, not the king the Lord had in mind for Israel. Wouldn't you just know that his name means "asked for," or "prayed for?" God is so into detail!

How about the names, Hopni and Phinehas, (the two evil sons of Eli), who were priests, (1 Samuel 1:3) and did wicked and evil in the sight of the Lord (1 Samuel 2:22-25). Hopni means a boxer and a swordsman. Phinehas literally means a serpent's mouth or brazen mouth (mouth of brass). Please read more about Hopni and Phinehas in 1 Samuel 2:27-36 and chapters 3-4 to see how their names lived up to their reputation.

Dez and I chose to speak Life into our children through their names, and the rewards have been immeasurable. Sometimes I call them by their first, middle, or last names; it depends on where I discern (by way of Holy Spirit) as to where they need improvement.

Knowing that meaning of words matter, we also made it a passion of ours never to call our sons "kids." I think that word has become the "in thing" today, but the word "kid" is only used in the Bible as a young goat (being sacrificed, or eaten)—it's not used to mean a child. In Webster's 1828 dictionary, "kid" also means a young goat, along with other meanings. Our sons and daughters are human beings not animals. (God is so gracious in revealing details of strategies for us to live the overcoming life). Therefore, I prefer to refer to them as daughters, sons, or children.

In the same vein, Dez and I did not tolerate name calling (using derogatory names) with our sons and their friends, nor from them, for obvious reasons.

Resources for Name Research

1. Dorothy Astoria, *The Name Book* (Minneapolis: Bethany House Publishers, 1982,1997, Revised and updated by Christopher J. Soderstrom.

2. Sarah M. Peterson (editor), *The Book of Names*, (Wheaton: Tyndale House, 1997).

Father, I thank you that you love us and call us by our names. I pray that parents will continue to seek your face concerning the naming of their children, that they will know what is the hope and calling that you have ordained for each precious child.

Lord God, I say thank you for names that give inclination to purpose, destiny, and calling; I thank you Lord for life, joy and wholeness being expressed in every name. I thank you for each child being a reflection of Christ Jesus in character. Thank you Holy Spirit for showing us the meaning to our lives in Messiah Jesus.

So great is my veneration for the Bible;
that the earlier my children begin
to read it the more confident will be my hopes
that they will prove useful citizens to their country
and respectable members of society.
~ John Quincy Adams
Sixth President
of the United States

Watering Your Sapling (Guided by Holy Spirit)

Cool, peaceful, refreshing; the colors were smashing, too: beautiful aquas and shades of blue came crashing down on me like a waterfall. I woke up, got out of bed, and waddled to the kitchen.

"I dreamt I was being drenched in water, and it felt so good," I said to my mother.

She looked down at me and said, "Cathy, your water just broke!" She grabbed a beach towel and wrapped it around me like a diaper. She woke Dez, and we were on our way. As I waited my turn, it seemed like my whole Lamaze class went into labor at the same time. I heard women screaming, so I stopped praying the 121st Psalm for myself and interceded for all the ladies who seemed to be in so much pain.

For me, the delivery of our first son was just like the Lamaze instructor said it would be. The labor was short, and I literally had no pain. Of course, Dez was such a wonderful coach.

Dezmond, our beloved son, arrived Saturday morning at 9:59 a.m. weighing in at 8 pounds, 13 ½ ounces and measuring 22 inches long, with a full head of wavy coal-black hair. He was the most beautiful baby I had ever laid eyes on. He didn't scream; he just let out a soft "heh" and a smile while I talked to him.

Dez laid his hand on him just as he did again with Dominick five years later while escorting them to the nursery (after counting fingers and toes). Dez's moment of joy had come because he had asked the Lord for sons, and this was a great beginning.

I read the Bible to Dezmond while he was in my womb; every day, I watered him with the Word. Every day, I told him his name, the meaning (gracious protector, youthful, and refreshing), and told him who he was in the Lord. We had quite a rapport going even before he made his debut.

After his birth, Holy Spirit impressed on me to buy children's books that showed positive images of American young males of African descent. I asked Holy Spirit why He had me do this, and His reply was that He wanted our sons to love themselves for the skin He put them in. WOW!

Every time their birthdays and Christmas came, the first thing on my gift list were children's books. I ordered them from a special store in Maryland, San Antonio, and especially Indianapolis. These books always depicted children being positive role models, with great character, integrity, and being joyful in life. We always bought books that displayed different cultural groups because it is important to teach children about the diversity of God's children, and to respect all children regardless of skin color (ethnicity) or physical abilities.

By the time they were older, we had approximately two hundred books, which we donated to libraries of the Christian Schools they went to. Parents really appreciated them.

Searching for "The" School

Dezmond was going on four years of age when we began looking for his first school.

"Dez, I think this school is New Age," I said as we eased ourselves through the door. The teacher talked about nothing but mother earth and seemed to put all religions in the same basket with no Truth as we know it. We had visited ten schools after finally deciding on a Christian school, which continued the teaching we taught at home.

If you don't homeschool, please become pro-active in the schools your children attend. Consider making surprise visits; we did it all the time throughout our sons' school years, even at the Christian schools, and I'm so glad we did. One day, when Dezmond was in the second grade, in walked this man in his military camouflage uniform—Dez. He heard what the children were listening to on the TV, walked to the VCR, took out the tape, went directly to the director, and said, "I don't pay for my son to go to school and aftercare for him to watch movies with cuss words in them."

This particular child's movie had about two or three cuss words in it, but the point was (and still is) if a school says it's Christian, where's the fruit? When I arrived to pick Dezmond up from school, the director told me what had happened and was very apologetic. It never happened again!

One of the most beautiful things you as parents can participate in with the Lord is to not only pray for your own children, but also the administration of the schools they attend, each child's teacher (by name), and the other children in the school. Think about this! Do you understand how many lives could be changed if we understood the magnitude of this principle? Let your children see you praying for their teachers, and let them even pray with you.

So many decisions have to be made about raising your children during their formative years. I pray that you make choices of life for your children because the decisions you make today, such as who is teaching your children, affect multitudes of generations:

> Listen, my people, to my teaching; turn your ears to the words from my mouth. I will speak to you in parables and explain mysteries from days of old. The things which we have known, and which our fathers told us we will not hide from their descendants; we will tell the generations to come the praises of ADONAI and his strength, the wonders that he has performed (Psalm 78:1-4 CJB).

When Father God looks at a family, He sees all the progeny in a family line, and so should we.

Raising Godly Siblings

"Ladies first," the young Dezmond said as he opened the door for me and the nurse to walk through. He was almost five years old when we arrived at the ob-gyn's office to check on his little brother. It always brought such a big grin to his face as he listened intently to the heartbeat. "That's my brother!" he would say.

We made a point to take him to every one of the doctor's visits, and do you know why? We wanted to make sure that the triplets (envy, jealously, and competition) didn't rear their ugly heads in our household. I've seen too many children, including my own siblings, fall for these culprits. These destructive spirits were in the first family in the Bible, too. The only way to rid a family line of them is to become diligent in teaching the Word of God to each child, train them in their purpose (according to what the Lord has created them for), and stay tuned in to Holy Spirit to catch concerns we as parents may miss.

An ounce of prevention and being pro-active go a long way in heading off the triplets and what could later turn into rejection by one of the siblings. We taught Dezmond how to be a godly big brother through prayer and the positive reinforcement he received from me and Dez. It worked. Dezmond immediately took on the role as protector to our faithful disciple, Dominick.

Dominick (belonging to the Lord, faithful disciple, victorious spirit, born on Sunday) made his heroic entrance three weeks late, 23 August 1987 on a Sunday at 10:10 a.m. He weighed in at 8 pounds, 12 ½ ounces, and was 21 ½ inches long, screaming his head off after trying to return to the womb. The doctor ended up grabbing him with forceps so that he wouldn't do his disappearing act.

What a complete difference from our firstborn! He was cute as a button with a peculiar temperament, an extremely active baby born for such a time as this. He is the son that I sang spiritual songs from the Lord to, and guess what? He has a joyful disposition (most of the time), and he loves to rejoice especially in the morning hour. Dominick has always been my "hold me close full of hugs" son, and Dezmond has stayed true to his name—gracious protector—and has maintained the godly role of big brother ever since.

Does It Really Take a Village?

"It takes a village to raise a child." I've pondered and pondered over this idea because I know that, as parents, we are responsible for establishing morals, principles, and virtue in our children. So what exactly does this saying mean? I believe "the village" is God's favor, mercy, and His kindness on our children's lives. He has divinely set in place certain people to extend to our sons and daughters His favor. Some will be teachers, mentors, spiritual mothers and fathers, who will add to (notice I said *add to*) what has already been established by the parents.

Whether your child received a certain scholarship, or a tutor when needed, let me say again: *the village is never to take the place of the parents unless there are no functional parents!*

Realizing that certain village members are important to the well-being of her children, my mother used to send my teachers presents with thank-you notes to let them know how much they were appreciated. We have followed this teaching in our family.

When our youngest son received his bachelor's degree, we held a dinner and purposely invited those who had been a blessing to him from God.

To each one, we sent the card below:

> Thank you for being the favor in our son's life! For every word of encouragement, reminding him who he is, and for every ounce of blessing that came from Father God through you, we say thank you. We decree in your life Numbers 6:24-27:
>
> > The Lord bless you and watch, guard, and keep you; The Lord make His face to shine upon and enlighten you and be gracious (kind, merciful, and giving favor) to you, The Lord lift up His (approving) countenance upon you and give you peace (tranquility and life continually).

As parents, we need to always show acts of kindness to those the Lord puts in place to show forth His favor in helping our children. They were already written in God's plan for your children before they were ever born. With that in mind, consider that it isn't so much the whole village who makes sure your children receive everything they are supposed to receive for their destiny in the Lord; rather, it's the plan of God working through people.

Root Out the Weeds

In researching the olive tree, I found that they survive much better if they have good weed control. In the root system of the lives of children, I call the weeds "invaders of the welfare of a growing child—intruders." In a child's life, uprooting weeds are important, but we have to remember we need to pour in all the more love, Bible teaching, virtues, communication, time, and discipline to keep the weeds away.

I recall when Dominick had a young lady friend in high school who liked him. When Dez and I met the young lady, we both discerned she was an "Oh No!" Holy Spirit placed in our hearts to start praying for her in love. We started praying for the young lady because we knew that the Lord loved her, too.

Within days, Dominick came home and said, "Mom, today I had a headache, and I told "SOS" about it, and she said she had something that would rid me of my headache.

"And what did she tell you?" I asked.

"Sex with her!"

Within one week of continued prayer, Holy Spirit had removed her out of his life! Thank you Lord! Even with that relief, we still continued to hold her name up to Holy Spirit praying for her change of heart and well being. Ask Holy Spirit to put it in your heart to pray for everyone and everything around your children. This includes people with different mindsets, attitudes, and all those who act like they might not like or love your child.

Remember to give your time to other children, care for them, and offer monetary gifts (for orphans) and, yes, sometimes give of your home to a child who may need a place of refuge. We have sometimes had a small platoon at our house because of Dominick; he is known for having a troop around him at all times, and I'm not talking only at birthday parties.

Father expects us to keep places in our hearts for other children He brings across our paths. So, every Wednesday, Dez and I fasted and prayed for our sons and for their friends. We have also cooked for, advised, and loved many children in the process of raising our children, and they have been mostly males.

Instead of being in fear about what life holds for our children, let's commit to root out the weeds and yet develop, teach, and instruct in the area of godly virtues. This is called being and operating from an offensive stance so that our children will be well-prepared for life.

> Planting, pouring in, and establishing in a child that which is godly is most important; that in itself will cause the bad to be uprooted.
>
> -- Mary Catherine R. Ard'is

Develop a Strong Root System

It was a glorious fall day in 2008. The foliage on the trees were turning into the most brilliant colors I had ever seen (fall is my favorite time of the year). The leaves turned gold, green, and red. Dez and I were shopping during this season when I spotted some tropical croton plants with those same colors. I thought they would look so nice in my plant bed. I must have bought seven pots, each one containing groups of three stems. I separated the stems and planted them in different spots in the plant bed.

The Tuesday after I planted them, the weather got cooler, and the season's first frost fell upon us. The plants weakened. Then the second frost came, and within a week they all died. Why? The plants did not have a chance to be rooted, grounded, acclimated, or established in the environment. They had no support system because I separated them and took the plants from the pots and put them in the ground. The surroundings were so strange to them that the roots didn't survive. These type of plants last longer when they are planted in the early spring in the same potted group so that they will become acclimated to the soil, and establish a good root system. When the frost comes, the leaves may die off, but because of the strong root system, it will bring forth new leaves the following year.

Why am I telling you this? Parents, be sure you give your children a strong root system before you release them into the world. Anchor them and make sure you are the two stakes tied to the young sapling as he or she is growing up. Give them the type of love and support that establishes them in who they are in the LORD.

Rely on Holy Spirit

An African Proverb reads, "Bend the twig while it is young," which essentially means "mothers and fathers, train and instruct; and added to this, establish that which is godly (good) for your children while they are young." A godly family life prepares your children for success in every sphere of life.

In marriage, we hold fast to the wisdom of Ecclesiastes 4:12: "A threefold cord [husband, wife, God] is not easily broken," and the same can go for parenthood. Raising godly children requires synergy among the child, parents, village, Father, Son, and Holy Spirit working together, realizing that it is Holy Spirit that truly provides the empowerment of godly parenthood.

Even a single parent with the help of Holy Spirit can raise children who are well established in the Lord to go out and do great exploits. Holy Spirit is the missing link, but we so often overlook Him as we raise our children. Frankly, without Him there is no success in rearing a child. My mother had to depend on Holy Spirit and He would always let her know when something was not going well with her children. All of us have to learn to depend, trust, and rely on the Spirit of God after all He is the Helper, Teacher (who leads us into all Truth) and our Comforter.

Father, I thank you for sending Holy Spirit to us, guiding us into all Truth. Grant to us as parents the knowledge of who You are. Let us experience the person and power of Holy Spirit in our lives, for You hold the keys, the perfect keys to raising daughters and sons according to the uniqueness in which You have created them.

Holy Spirit, You care about every detail concerning raising these precious gifts You have entrusted to us. Teach us Holy Spirit about every thing You desire for our children. Lead us into all truths concerning them, realizing that You know all things.

We submit ourselves to You as a child submits to a parent trusting that with You all things are possible (Mark 11:24) and You are not a man that You should lie; if You've said it, then You will do it (Numbers 23:19). Teach us Holy Spirit how to raise sons and daughters who will always rely on You as they would their very breath. Not our will but Yours be done in the mighty name of Christ Jesus, Yeshua our Messiah.

> I will ask the Father, and He will give you another Comforter (Counselor, Helper, Intercessor, Advocate, Strengthener, and Standby), that He may remain with you forever—The Spirit of Truth, Whom the world cannot receive (welcome, take to its heart), because it does not see Him or know and recognize Him. But you know and recognize Him, for He lives with you [constantly] and will be in you. I will not leave you as orphans [comfortless, desolate, bereaved, forlorn, helpless]; I will come [back] to you (John 14:16-18).

An aware parent loves all children
he or she interacts with—for you are a caregiver
for those moments in time.
~ Doc Childre
American development specialist
and the founder of the Heart Math Institute

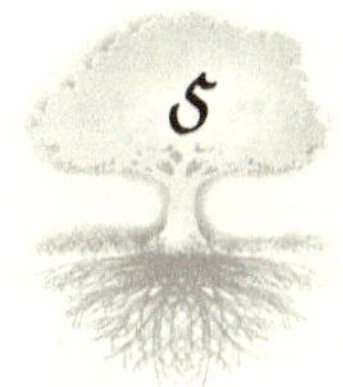

Tending Your Young Plant (Be an Example)

A child is born to us this day, may God teach her in His way.

~ Clethann L. Jones Rutherford
Mother of Author

I've often looked at the words above and asked Father, "What exactly did You put on my mother's heart when she wrote those words in my baby book?" I've viewed them as my very own blessing my mother prayed when I was born. I now know when I first asked the question to Father that she was asking Holy Spirit to be my teacher, my counselor, comforter, guide, friend, and much more.

My mother embodied the Proverbs 31 lady--a lady of excellence. If you listened to her wise counsel, you would never go astray. She set a godly example for her children, nieces, nephews, and grandchildren. And in my adulthood, she was my very best friend. I understand now more than ever what she really gave up in her life for my two sisters, my brother, and me. My parents divorced when I was in the fourth grade, and she never got married again nor did she date. She went home to be with the Lord on 1 July 1997. I held her (and still do) in the highest esteem and honor. This chapter is dedicated to her memory.

"Create a taste for God in the heart of your child and when he is old he will not depart from it."

"That's it!" I said turning quickly to see Dr. Ron Hembree speaking on his TV show, "Quick Study." I realized that's exactly the road Holy Spirit has for all parents. The question remains, how do we accomplish this feat? I know this one thing, parents: we have to allow the virtues that are in our Lord to be in us by Holy Spirit.

Everything that our Lord is, that's what we allow to grow in us by the power of Holy Spirit. His formation in us is then seen by our children; we call it the Fruit of the Spirit. Dez and I have learned as parents that we think we know it all, but we are inclined to agree with one of Job's friends, Elihu, who said, "Age should speak, and a multitude of years should teach wisdom [so let it be heard]. But there is [a vital force] a spirit [of intelligence] in man, and the breath of the Almighty gives men understanding. It is not the great [necessarily] who are wise, nor [always] the aged who understand justice" (Job 32:7-9).

You see, the two go hand in hand: wisdom and understanding of all age groups. On one hand, our sons taught us love, patience, sacrifice, understanding, compassion, joy, and much more. On the other hand, we taught our children wisdom, love, compassion, sharing, and relying on Holy Spirit. We didn't realize, though, how much our teaching would remain in them and be put into action during some of the most trying times in our family.

A Family Doubles in a Day

Dez's last military assignment before he retired brought us to Riyadh, the capital city of Saudi Arabia. There, Dez served in OPM-SANG (U.S. Army Office of the Program Manager) as part of a diplomatic advisor team from July 1991 to August 1994. Many of you may remember that the first Gulf War ended in May of 1991. So, for me, that assignment turned into the best we ever had because we got a chance to really spend quality time together as a family.

My husband has always been quite adventurous and wanted his sons to be exposed to different cultures. He got his wish in Riyadh where almost every nation is represented in the city and even in the piano classes I taught. I loved being amidst such diversity; it fulfilled a childhood wish since the time I read a set of books entitled *Lands and Peoples* from Grolier Encyclopedias. I remember telling Mother, "I'm going here and here; you just watch and see." And so I did.

While we were in Saudi, Dez planned our first month-long family vacation; he decided to take us to Kenya in East Africa on Safari. Dominick loved animals, and just for the adventure of it, we all wanted to go. Both sons enjoyed the trip, and it gave us the opportunity to become closer as a family. After safariing, we spent three weeks traveling to different nations to see how other people lived.

We moved back to the states in August 1994, to Tallahassee, Florida, which was the last place on our list we wanted to settle, but Father knows best (Tallahassee is a great city to raise children); and when Father says this is the place I want you, well, what can you do or say?

We continued to grow even closer as a family unit. Dez and I took turns volunteering at the Christian schools our sons went to, keeping a close watch on them to get them acclimated to living in the states again. We started going to Christian conferences in and out of town, and we became ministers of children, youth, and young adults in the church we attended.

Life, however, rarely goes without incident. In January of 1997, my mother was diagnosed with pulmonary fibrosis, then cancer from her many years of smoking. So, Dez and I pursued buying a house in the Orlando area, where she lived. We wanted to keep both of our mothers and my youngest sister's three sons in our home.

One weekend in April, while we were in Orlando looking at houses, mother had a relapse. We didn't have the heart to leave her there while we were back in Tallahassee, so we packed her up and brought her home with us. Mother got progressively worse, so I'm glad I could be with her to make sure that she was being well cared for until she passed on July 1. This didn't relieve our family from our appointed assignments, though. Our next mission stared us straight in our face.

My baby sister (the mother of Joshua and Jacob) was suffering from a severely broken heart, deep postpartum depression (that she never came out of), a legalistic church, and a truckload of the spirit of rejection (an eighteen wheeler full and then some). She had been committed to two different mental hospitals, and she was taking psychotropic prescription drugs, which she hated. These drugs affect the central nervous system and can be mind altering. She would stop taking them at times because of the way they made her feel, but then she'd go to crack cocaine to feel better about herself. It was the meanest most vicious circle I had ever seen, changing her mood in an instant.

It seemed like the adversary had sucked the very life out of my sister, whom I loved dearly. If I only knew in 1979 what I know now—how to apply the strategies of the Lord in spiritual warfare and everything else our Lord taught in the four gospels). In other words, if I only knew how to set the captives free, but I didn't. So, all I could do was hold her and love her, cry like a big baby, and pray. She had been living like this since October 1979, the week of my wedding. I moved her to Orlando from the first hospital in 1980, and I stayed there to help my mother while Dez was in Fort Drum, New York.

I needed to go back in time and paint a picture for you to understand the home environment of my nephews before they came to live with us. Whenever their mom came back from the mental hospital or from jail, the entire atmosphere of the home changed from peaceful to chaotic. I know it felt like a living hell for my mother and nephews, so Joshua Allen and Jacob Michael (identical twins) who had lived with my mother for fourteen years, came to live with us the week before mother passed. They were extremely attached to her, had no father figure, and now had no mother figure they could rely on. Their older brother, Chris, decided to live with another family because of his football endeavors, so Joshua and Jacob became our assignment from Father.

When they were younger, my sister and I kept going back and forth on us adopting them. One minute she would say, yes, and the next moment she would change her mind. Now, they were fourteen going on fifteen (Dezmond's age), six foot tall, and skinny as string beans.

Dez and I wondered how we would integrate our nephews into our family and really make them feel as though they always belonged. We also needed God's wisdom on how to deal with and confront the issues they had because of their childhood. We wondered how we would deal with the shame they must have felt from being picked at by neighbors and classmates because of their mother's condition. We also had to face dealing with the spirit of poverty because my sister impoverished my mother's household to feed her drug addiction.

Dez and I were also concerned about how to maintain what we already had taught our two sons and at the same time be fair to everyone involved. These issues and others plagued my heart and mind because I had to deal with my separation from my mother on top of all this.

I want to tell you what a trooper I have for a husband! He immediately stepped in and said to me, the Lord says, "I'm suppose to take them in as my own sons."

But that wasn't their plan. Jacob and Joshua said we were too strict. They wanted to continue to live as they had been living, so they visited some of their relatives and friends in Orlando to see if they could stay with them. It's so funny to say this now, but every relative and friend they went to said, "I can take one but not both of you," or "I don't want this one because he has a nasty attitude."

You see, the Lord had a plan to preserve their lineage all along, so they had no choice; the blueprint for their life was already in place, and God was the designer in charge. So, we all sat down and talked. Dez offered to give them his last name, but they wanted to keep their mother's last name, which is also my maiden name. We had no idea who their daddy was at the time; we only heard he had died of lupus. We figured we could do more research on that later. Jacob and Joshua didn't want to be adopted either, so we retained a lawyer to work out legal guardianship papers.

Dez did not want me to work at that time because we were going to need someone to pick everybody up from school and monitor homework, plus take care of other things. I thought that I was real close to FATHER, but during that time after mother had passed, I soaked in the presence of the Lord, cried, and sang so much that He healed me completely. I couldn't find it in me at that time to move to Orlando, so we all stayed in Tallahassee. It took me almost three years to even make a visit.

Tend with Boundaries

Setting an example includes setting boundaries and sticking to them, especially in tough situations. As a new family, we had issues to work out. The last week my mother lived, Dezmond, Dominick, Joshua, and Jacob were at the breakfast table eating. Dez sat down and asked, "Where's the food, Mary?"

"I put it all on the table. I thought you had eaten." I said.

After one week and a $500 grocery bill, Dez and I had to come to a meeting of the minds concerning food and other issues with our nephews/sons. You see, Jacob and Joshua were used to thinking,"Eat all you can because there might not be any later." So, to ensure that what I cooked for two days would last for two days, they and the entire family were each allowed two helpings per plate because "Mommy" had other things to do than just cook 24/7. They could have all they wanted to eat at the buffet we went to once a month.

Joshua and Jacob thought that taking lunches to school meant they were poor, so they paid for their lunches. They were taught by me and Dez that, when given a choice, they had to stick with their decision no matter what it was. We would tell them, "decide carefully by weighing your options not by what someone else is doing." They wanted to change their minds when they saw what scrumptious lunches I prepared for their cousins, but Jacob and Joshua stuck to their decision and continued to pay for their lunches.

This simple "stick to your decision" rule cut down the triplets of competition, envy, and jealousy between all the boys, but like most families with teenagers, we still faced issues. About a month after they came to live with us, I needed to go shopping. In the past, I had always left Dezmond in charge. This time, Joshua made an ardent appeal: "Aunt Cathy, you always leave Dezmond in charge," he said. "How come I can't be in charge? I know what to do. You can trust me."

And so I said, "Okay, everyone knows the rules."

When I returned home, I noticed an unusual quiet. "How did everything go?" I asked.

"Okay," they all said.

But you know we moms have that prophetic sense that tells us, "Uh uh, not in this lifetime!" When I took them all to the store, Dezmond told me what happened because I pressured him. He hated to tell on his cousins, but he knew his parents well. While I was gone, they (Jacob and Joshua) played video games and started cussing. I was livid!

After that incident, I could count on Dominick to tell me everything because he was the baby of them all and, at that time, he loved to tattle. Well, Pop came home and we put the video games away for a month, or until they grew out of the cussing syndrome.

About a month after that, the minivan episode happened. Jacob and Joshua hated the back seat because of how they saw themselves. Dezmond and Dominick knew who they were since the time they were in the womb, so it didn't matter to them what seat they rode in.

I say all of this to let you know how heavy the spirit of rejection covered them. We prayed for God's wisdom, understanding, and knowledge to come forth on Joshua and Jacob, so they would receive His ways to handle their problems.

I'm thankful this day that the Lord had given us specific steps in raising Dezmond and Dominick so that our nephews' issues weren't compounded when they came to live with us. When we all get together now, they laugh about Dominick tattling on them and how Jacob and Joshua used to try to beat him up when I left the house, but never really succeeded.

At the time, though, our Jacob (the one who dealt with rejection the most from his birth mom) didn't laugh much. He had meningitis as a baby and became hurt and angry a lot. He would even challenge me when I asked him to do his chores. That spirit of rejection and even rebellion would ping pong off the two of them.

Dez and I knew Father's ways still had to be taught to them with an abundance of compassion and love, so Dezmond, Dominick, Jacob, and Joshua all started their mornings at five-thirty with devotion from Proverbs with Dez, and then they would get ready for school. If anyone fell asleep they would have to stand up, read aloud the Proverb, and expound on it.

Whenever Dez talked to Jacob, he would cry, (mainly because he had never had a father figure in his life, and Dez's military training gave him a voice of authority), so we realized we had to exercise a lot of understanding, gentle talking, and explaining with him. Joshua, on the other hand, could rationalize his way out of any talking we did with him. Now, this is where the Fruit of the Spirit helps immeasurably in raising children, especially with older children. While Dez and I were fasting, praying, and co-laboring with Holy Spirit on their behalf, Father began to work overtime on their attitudes and how they felt in general about having to comply with boundaries. We saw the effects of our efforts increase through their high school years. It helped greatly that our nephews were still pure (sexually) when they came to live with us, and that in itself was a huge blessing.

They left our home after high school because they wanted to be all grown up while in college, but they listened to our instructions, and teachings and did not turn away from them or from the Lord. I'm not saying they were perfect; I am saying Father had created in them a place in their hearts for Him, and if they did depart they soon returned to Him. For that we are so grateful, more than you will ever know.

The efforts certainly paid off. Joshua graduated from college with his degree in Graphic Design and Jacob in Graphic Communications Management. They love the Lord, both are married to beautiful wives (Kaneisha and Mary) who also love the Lord, and they both have children. Joshua has two daughters (Jania and Jaala), and Jacob has a daughter and a son (Amina and Jabari).

Joshua is a branch bank manager, and Jacob works as a systems project analyst. It's beautiful when the plan of the Lord comes to fruition in a person's life. And I know that He has not completed His work in them. Even as I write this, tears stream down my face because the Lord was and still is with them. Father indeed had a plan. He chose us to execute His plan with Holy Spirit taking the lead; we just followed.

> God places the solitary in families and gives the desolate a home in which to dwell; He leads the prisoners out to prosperity; but the rebellious dwell in a parched land (Psalm 68:6).

Tend with Purpose and Posterity

Parents, don't be in a hurry for your children to grow up and leave home, and don't look upon them as burdens. Children are a heritage of the Lord (Psalm 127:3). Like the name of this book, God says they are precious, highly prized, rare, and original cargo entrusted to you. In all the people that have been on the face of the earth and are still and yet to come, there has never been another like them, even with identical twins. That, parents, is the handiwork of the One we serve, and He gives His precious creation as a gift to you, so you can help His gift flourish and accomplish what He has purposed for them.

King David had a purpose, a vision, something he wanted to do in his lifetime--build a house for the Ark of the Lord (1 Chronicles 17), but Father had something else in mind, and it was much deeper than that. The word "house" dealt with posterity, David's lineage.

I have to quote the entire chapter for you because it's so awesome to read how the LORD gave David something more than a building. God gave him something that every family should long for.

> As David sat in his house, he said to Nathan the prophet, Behold, I dwell in a house of cedars, but the ark of the covenant of the Lord remains under tent curtains. Then Nathan said to David, Do all that is in your heart, for God is with you. And that same night the word of God came to Nathan, saying, Go and tell David My servant, Thus says the Lord: You shall not build Me a house to dwell in, for I have not dwelt in a house since the day that I brought up Israel from Egypt until this day; but I have gone from tent to tent, and from one tabernacle to another. Wherever I have walked with all Israel, did I say a word to

any of the judges of Israel whom I commanded to feed My people, saying, Why have you not built Me a house of cedar?

Now therefore, thus shall you say to My servant David, Thus says the Lord of hosts: I took you from the sheepfold, from following the sheep, that you should be prince over My people Israel. And I have been with you wherever you have gone, and I have cut off all your enemies from before you, and I will make your name like the name of the great ones of the earth. Also I will appoint a place for My people Israel and will plant them, that they may dwell in their own place and be moved no more; neither shall the children of wickedness waste them any more, as at the first, since the time that I commanded judges to be over My people Israel. Moreover, I will subdue all your enemies.

Furthermore, I foretell to you that the Lord will build you a house (a blessed posterity). And it shall come to pass that when your days are fulfilled to go to be with your fathers, I will raise up your offspring after you, one of your own sons, and I will establish his kingdom. He shall build Me a house, and I will establish his throne forever.

I will be his father, and he shall be My son; and I will not take My mercy and steadfast love away from him, as I took it from him [King Saul] who was before you. But I will settle him (Him) in My house and in My kingdom forever; and his (His) throne shall be established forevermore.

According to all these words and according to all this vision, so Nathan spoke to David. And David the king went in and sat before the Lord and said, Who am I, O Lord God, and what is my house and family, that You have brought me up to this?

And yet this was a small thing in Your eyes, O God; for You have spoken of Your servant's house for a great while to come, and have regarded me according to the estate of a man of high degree, O Lord God! What more can David say to You for thus honoring Your servant? For You know Your servant.

O Lord, for Your servant's sake and in accord with Your own heart, You have wrought all this greatness, to make known all these great things. O Lord, there is none like You, nor is there any God beside You, according to all that our ears have heard. And what nation on the earth is like Your people Israel, whom God went to redeem to Himself as a people, making Yourself a name by great and terrible things, by driving out nations from before Your people, whom You redeemed out of Egypt?

You made Your people Israel Your own forever, and You, Lord, became their God. Therefore now, Lord, let the word which You have spoken concerning Your servant and his house be established forever, and do as You have said.

Let it be established and let Your name [and the character that name denotes] be magnified forever, saying, The Lord of hosts, the God of Israel, is Israel's God; and the house of David Your servant will be established before You. For You, O my God, have told Your servant that You will build for him a house (a blessed posterity); therefore Your servant has found courage and confidence to pray before You.

And now, Lord, You are God, and have promised this good thing to Your servant. **Therefore may it please You to bless the house (posterity) of Your servant, that it may continue before You forever; for what You bless, O Lord, is blessed forever. (emphasis mine.)**

Let's take a pause, a Selah moment, a praise break, and meditate on how wonderful our God is!

As we read the chapter, we see how David's desires to build a home for the ark are filled with the right heart attitude. David did not get upset with Father for allowing his son (Solomon) to build the Temple instead of him. David even helped his son by preparing everything he needed for him to build it (1 Chronicles 22, 28; 29:1-9).

Abraham also provided Isaac with all that he needed because he was "the son of promise" (Genesis 25:5).

Even after Hannah left her son with Eli to be in the service of the Lord, she continued to make robes for Samuel and take the garments to him once a year (1 Samuel 2:19). Monoah asked that the Lord once again tell him (he had already told his wife) how to raise the baby Samson once he was born (Judges 13).

How about John the Baptist (Luke 1: 5-25, 57-79)? His parents followed the instruction of the Lord to the letter.

And Jesus (Yeshua), the purpose for which the great book (the Bible) was written, tells the story of how His parents, Joseph and Mary fled to Egypt to save His life even though Joseph was not Jesus' natural father. However, Joseph operated as an extension of the Father and stood in God's stead.

In every case, the parents followed God's will for their children's lives. Father desires to build a posterity in our familes also that lives on down the generational lines. Therefore, ask your children questions to get them thinking how the Lord would want them to live their lives. Do whatever it takes to raise your child in the fear and admonition of the Lord and propel them forward into the role the Lord wants them to fulfill. Do not neglect the spiritual side nor the natural because they work hand in hand. Their education should always begin in the home because we are the first line of teachers our children are introduced to and, therefore, we take the lead spiritually and intellectually.

The formative years (the womb to six years of age) is the time we want to spend pouring into our children everything they will need for the spiritual as well as the natural. Developing and creating those unforgettable moments in life, communicating and listening at all times so that when children mature, they'll want to talk to us about anything, no matter what their age. It will become natural to them because they started at a young age.

Tend with Gifts for God

When we lived in Saudi Arabia, I was thinking one day about Christmas (the day we celebrate the Lord's birth) and an idea came to me. We remember as children how our parents would ask, "What do you want for your birthday?" Well, I felt the commercialism of Christmas had made the holiday seem like a time to get and get more things. So Dez and I got our ten- and five-year-old guys together and posed this question to them: "Since it is JESUS' birthday, don't you think we ought to ask Him what He wants for His birthday?"

Now you know they wanted to say no, but we had them think about it, and that's how we got them down to receiving only one gift from us at Christmas. The one gift symbolized what a gift the Lord became for us when He came into the world. We then had them participate in giving to children who did not have what they had, like clean water, clothes, books, etc. Dez and I were already giving these things, but it was time they learned also.

Did we celebrate the Easter bunny? No. We did not because it is not the reason for the season. Do we ever celebrate Halloween? No. Never! Why celebrate fear? We did not want anything to come between Father and His sons which He gave to us (I John 5:21).

In trying to set a godly example, did Dez and I blunder sometimes? Yes, we did and so we changed our way to conform to His ways (Isaiah 55:8). God has given us choices, and if you did not train up your child at an early age, fear not because our Abba (Father God) in all His glory and splendor is faithful in His grace and mercy to woo our children, even when we raise them in ignorance: "My people perish for lack of knowledge. "

That word "knowledge" deals with knowing God. In knowing Him, we become aware and acquainted with His ways and choose life. He is very true, and He desires you to choose life so that you and your descendants will live and have that God-kind of life.

Let Them See
(A Declaration to Parents)

Let your children see you bow down, prostrate yourselves before the Mighty God (EL-GIBOR), God Most High (EL-ELYON) in the reverential fear of the Lord in worship (2 Chronicles 20:18).

Let them see you depend on Him for everything (Proverbs 3:5).

Let them see you wait on the Lord with no anxiety, knowing that His timing is perfect (Isaiah 40:31).

Let them see you pray for them, interceding also for the ethnos (people groups) of the world (Isaiah 56:7)

Let them see you apologize when you are wrong, asking for forgiveness from Father, and set your way to repent (change your direction) (2 Samuel 12:14).

Let them see that you love your spouse and be true to your marriage covenant, observing the true beauty of marriage (Ephesians 5:31-33).

Let them see you honor and love your parents (Ephesians 6:1-3).

Let them see you put Father God, Christ Jesus, and Holy Spirit above every human and every thing on the face of the earth (Matthew 6:33 and Deuteronomy 6:5).

Let them see you love mankind no matter what and say as Jesus said, "Father forgive them for they know not what they do" (John 15: 12-13).

Let them see you give because so much has been given to you (Matthew 10:8).

Let them see you forgive because so much has been forgiven of you (Luke 7:47).

Let them see you be truthful because He is Truth (John 14:6).

Let them see you find your way because He is the Way (John 14:6).

Let them see you live the Zoe kind of life because He is Life (John 14:6).

Let them see you as a child of the Living God, our Father (Matthew 18:4; Mark 10:14; and Luke 18:17).

*My fruit is better than gold,
yes, than refined gold,
and my increase than choice silver.*
~ *Proverbs 8:19 AMP*

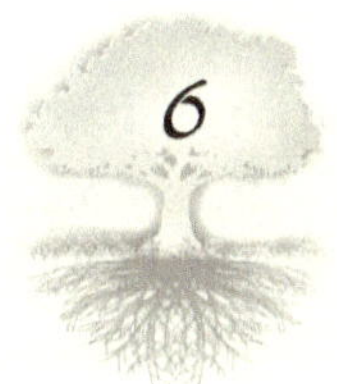

6

Basking in the Sonlight (Growing in the Presence of God)

We've talked up to this moment about the word "fruit" or *periy* in the Hebrew meaning "offspring" or the "fruit of the womb" as used in Psalm 127:3. In the rest of this book, I want to talk about fruit as in the Greek word *karpos,* which includes all kinds of "offspring" or "fruit of the womb," not just children.

One of its meanings is the visible expression of power working inwardly and invisibly through works and deeds. The character of the "fruit" is evidence of the character of the power producing it. That power is the indwelling of Holy Spirit.

We have included some of the fruit or characteristics of the Spirit of the Living God (Holy Spirit) in some of the previous prayers. This fruit is listed in Galatians 5:22 and are brought into us through our union with Christ Jesus. We must allow Holy Spirit to mature us into the character of Christ Jesus because the Fruit of the Spirit is what Yeshua (Jesus) embodied. It was His character and He longs to reproduce his character in us. Just as natural trees need the sunlight to grow, so we as spiritual trees need Sonlight to properly grow and produce fruit in our lives.

~ *Dis-Ease* ~

Without the SONlight, trees can grow up crooked
and go through life with no sense of direction,
believing anything and anybody that comes their way.
They may not know what they believe, if they believe.
In and out, round and about,
somebody help, help me please;
I need the SON to ease this dis-ease.
Somebody help, help me please.
Did I sign a lease for this dis-ease?
Somebody help, help me please
and don't you tease.
I need the SON to cease this dis-ease.

~ Mary Catherine R. Ard'is

Inside of so many youth is a cry to know the Son in all His glory. Parents, give your sons and daughters the opportunity to know Him in all His benefits (Psalm 103:2-5, 116:12-13).

The greatest thing we can teach our children is the unconditional love that Father God has for them. Our worship for Him is actually our lowliness in our heart-attitude. When we worship, we realize how awesome, great, and perfect Father is and how imperfect we are. It is in times of worship that we are able to recognize how much we need Him in everything we do.

When I worked at Disney World, I was taught how to spot counterfeit money by examining the real bill first. May you seek His face and find His solutions for all situations in life. Hear the "real" will of God then you can spot the "counterfeit."

How can you hear God if you don't know His voice? Spend time with Him first and foremost. Study how Father speaks; tune in to His frequency, and you will begin to hear His voice.

In the four Gospels, especially the book of John, we see the disciples listening to and learning from the Master Teacher Himself. This was their time to bask, to be like a sponge and soak up everything Jesus said and did. Jesus was not only teaching them the Word but demonstrating the Word by being the Word. In fact, the Pharisees complained to Yeshua (Messiah Jesus) that His disciples spent their time feasting instead of fasting. Jesus told them that as long as He (the Bridegroom) was with them, they did not need to fast. But when He leaves, they will fast in that day (Mark 2:19-20). You could say they spent the three years basking in the light of the SON.

Pray for your sons and daughters to hear and know the voice of Holy Spirit at a young age. It was evident that Dominick knew His voice the morning after my mother went home to be with the Lord in 1997. Dominick came rushing into our room early; he was so excited: "Mommy, I heard Nanny's voice. She was with the Lord, and she told me to be a good boy and obey my mommy and daddy. She said she was going away for a while and she would see me later."

I knew it was God in all His grace and mercy because the night my mother passed, Dominick had a difficult time. When we told him Nanny had passed on to Heaven, he cried himself to sleep; he was nine years old at the time.

I am sometimes asked, when should we introduce the Lord to our children for their salvation? How about whenever Holy Spirit tells you and them because you want them to remember that special day. Meanwhile pray 2 Timothy 2:10:

> I will "persevere and stand my ground with patience and endure everything for the sake of the elect [God's chosen], so that they too may obtain [the] salvation which is in Christ Jesus, with [the reward of] eternal glory."

Persevere in prayer; do not force your children to accept Jesus as their Savior because only Holy Spirit knows when they are ready, and He will let you know when they are ready, so rest (trust) in Him that they will know Him. That day arrived twice for both Dominick and Dezmond.

Listening to the guest speaker make an altar call one evening at church, my twelve-year old Dominick looked at me and said, "Mommy, I don't remember accepting the Lord as my personal Savior. I need to go up and accept Him." His pop and I tried to tell him when he did accept the Lord, but it was important that he remembered, too. So Dominick was the first person to walk down during the altar call and, to this day, he vividly remembers the night. Dezmond accepted the Lord at an early age of ten, but felt he needed to rededicate himself while he was away at college in his freshman year. You see how important it is for them to know Holy Spirit's voice?

As parents, we are never too mature in the faith to spend time learning to hear His voice more clearly. When Dez was offered the position in Riyadh, the Gulf War was getting ready to start, so Dez told them that he and I would pray about it. I want to tell you, we were given the "Yes, go" from the Lord, plus He gave me an added bonus when He told me the war would be over in May—and it was. Everyone thought we were crazy to go, but we had such a peace about it.

I was working for the government with plenty of overtime, and was juggling husband, sons, work, church, and having a zeal to know more about the Lord, so when everyone went to bed, I stayed up sometimes until three in the morning, praying, meditating on the Word or listening to different ministers teaching the Word. I spent my days off at our sons' schools volunteering, and we always participated in the weekend fundraising events. All of these activities caused me to become supermom, which was not good.

It was time to move again, and because I was so stressed and tired, I told Father that when we got to our new duty station, I was going to sit still and do only what He wanted me to do. They put me on a leave of absence from my old job, and off we went.

I still had not heard what He wanted for me, so I continued to sit still. We had been in Riyadh almost four months, and my administrative leave from my previous government job was coming to a close. I was offered a Management Analyst job, but I declined because I knew that was not what I was supposed to do, so I continued to pray and wait.

Dez came home after work and said, "Mary, you are going to lose your time-in–grade." I repeated to him what I had promised the Lord. He said, "Okay."

That Christmas, I became the director for the Children's Christmas program for two consecutive years. In January, I began teaching private piano lessons to students from many nations, and I became the president of the board for OPM-SANG's Child Development Center.

I learned to sit real still and spend all the time in the world with the Lord. I continually meditated on His Word, as well as other Christian books while riding to the different stores in what we called our limousine service. These cars were not limousines as we know them in the states, but were simply up-to-date cars. We were given this service because ladies are not permitted to drive in Saudi Arabia, nor sit in the front seat unless the driver is their husband.

I basked in the light of the Son so much those three years that He really fine tuned my relationship with Him taking it to another level. He developed that inner peace in me that passes all understanding. The peace of the Lord rested in our home, and it still does.

For this peace to be in your home, become a gatekeeper. Create a place in your home where Holy Spirit can dwell so the sweet fragrance of the Lord can permeate the atmosphere. There are certain things we just don't allow in our home, and our sons know what they are because we raised them to know. If you were God, would you want to live in a home where profanity is the norm? How about XXX rated movies, strife, jealously, competition, envy, statues of false deities, anger, madness, wrath, lying, murder, ugly heart conditions, cheating, dishonesty, no mercy, no grace?, How about no self-control, no integrity, rape, incest, lust, adultery, the pride of life, a proud look, and no salvation in the home? Would you want to dwell in such a loveless place? Well, neither does the Spirit of the Living God.

When the atmosphere is conducive to the dwelling of the Lord, it will be easy to hear His voice, learn about Him, keep Him in our hearts, and reap the benefits of our children keeping their relationship with Him. Children will also excel in their school work, have a peace that surrounds them, commune with Holy Spirit, know and hear what their purpose is, be inspired to keep the reverential fear of the Lord, His Precepts, His Word, and they will know who He is to them. Selah (pause and meditate).

Father, in the blessed and matchless name of Yeshua Messiah Jesus, I pray for the up close, personal, intimate relationship that these parents and their sons and daughters have with You. Father cause these relationships to grow. May their days be ordered of You so that they can have time for communing with You thereby ordering their days. Take away the anxieties and fears concerning the things of this life and teach them oh Lord that You and You alone hold the keys to what they need. Father, I thank You that You are still speaking today. We just need to make sure our frequency is where You are.

Thank You for girding them with strength for the journey, making their way perfect (Psalm 18), teaching their hands to war, setting them securely on the high places, and most of all for keeping their hearts pure before you. You are the Mighty God, God Most High, always there, full of grace, full of tender mercies for us. You are loving and kind; You are our Shalom (Peace), our Stronghold, Sure Foundation, Master, Lord, and King, Lion of Judah, Counselor, Spirit of the Living God, Our Banner,Great Shepherd, Alpha and Omega, Author and Finisher.

You complete everything You start, and we say thank You for the work You have started and, yet, are so faithful to complete in us. Amen.

The fruit
of the [uncompromisingly] righteous
is a tree of life, and he who is wise
captures human lives
[for God,as a fisher of men—
he gathers and receives them for eternity].
~ Proverbs 11:30 AMP

Delight in Golden Delicious Fruit (Fruit that Remains)

For this reason [seeing the greatness of this plan by which you are built together in Christ], I bow my knees before the Father of our Lord Jesus Christ,

For Whom every family in heaven and on earth is named [that Father from Whom all fatherhood takes its title and derives its name].

May He grant you out of the rich treasury of His glory to be strengthened and reinforced with mighty power in the inner man by the [Holy] Spirit [Himself indwelling your innermost being and personality].

May Christ through your faith [actually] dwell (settle down, abide, make His permanent home) in your hearts! May you be rooted deep in love and founded securely on love,

~ Ephesians 3:14-17

The Fruit of Love

I cannot dot another *i* or cross another *t* until I honor my daddy for allowing himself to be transformed by the renewing of his mind concerning his children.

Daddy had been a member of church all his life, but he became very selfish at one time in his life; and unfortunately, his children paid for his actions, especially in dealing with the turmoil that the divorce brought on our family.

Ironically, his favorite book in the Bible was Ecclesiastes, the book that's filled with Solomon's investigation of life and his conclusions that life matters only with the proper respect and reverential fear of the Lord, which leads to wisdom.

Daddy allowed himself to be strengthened in his inner man by the power of Holy Spirit; and in that strengthening, Father captured his heart, and he set out to make things right with his children. A total transformation occurred in his life as he became our daddy from Father, taking his cues from Father God Himself. He filled the last ten years of his life on earth apologizing from his heart to me and my siblings concerning his past actions. He even bared his soul to me over breakfast and on the phone, saying he was destined to preach the gospel, but he didn't answer the call; instead, the mantle had been passed to his baby brother. He was not only sorry for how he let us down but also how he let the Lord down.

Dad and Momma Louise (step-mom) moved back to Tallahassee a few years before we did. One day at his home, Daddy said to me, "Cathy, I have been reading this book and listening to these tapes on the Blessing that your sister, Marie, gave me. You're the first one of my children I've seen since I finished them, so let me lay my hands on your head and bless you!" And he did. This was the year 2002, and I was forty eight years young at the time.

I highly recommend that book to you, too: *Imparting the Blessings To Your Children: Your Biblical Heritage, What the Jewish Patriarchs Knew* by William T Ligon, Sr.

Father, in all His wisdom, knew that He wanted me to be completely reconciled with my earthly dad. That was part of His total plan for us moving back to Tallahassee—total restoration that included his blessing and getting all my questions answered.

Daddy went home to be with the Lord in March 2004, and I now have such precious and loving memories of him, I love him and embrace him because he is a part of who I am.

The story of my daddy and me is the perfect story of the Father's heart for redemption and restoration between all fathers and their children. Every parent, natural and spiritual, has to realize that Father does know best for all of us, and there is always a redemptive and restorative factor with Him.

Our Father is sovereign, and He knows your children better than you do. He knows what it will take to bring them to Him and to you.

I wrote this in dedication to the Father, who helped my daddy reconcile himself to us:

i needed

i needed daddy time
i needed FATHER's time
i needed to know that
HE loved me so
i needed daddy time
i needed FATHER's time

i needed to know that
HE would be all mine
i needed daddy time
i needed FATHER's time,
and still today
i need FATHER's time
time that shows me
i am all YOURS and YOU are mine;
i need my FATHER's time,
only YOU really know me
only YOU can show me
who i am and
why am i here
i need my FATHER's time,
In HIM
i have my meaning
On HIM
i am leaning
ABBA please show me, nobody ever told me
my days are all recorded,
every second written long ago
in a book with my very special name.
As i gain LIFE in YOU,
i will aim to stay in YOU
then i will have attained LIFE,
and LIFE more abundantly
i need my FATHER's time,
and as i looked around,
YOU were always there.

SELAH! Time for a praise break!

Father will always take everything and work it for our good (Romans 8:28). And that parents, you can take to the bank because His words are worth far more than gold and silver.

Our biggest accomplishment in life does not lie in things. Our accomplishments lie in our children and how we raise them up for the Lord; that is the fruit which will last throughout the generations.

> Blessed (happy, fortunate, prosperous, and enviable) is the man who walks and lives not in the counsel of the ungodly [following their advice, their plans and purposes], nor stands [submissive and inactive] in the path where sinners walk, nor sits down [to relax and rest] where the scornful [and the mockers] gather.
>
> But his delight and desire are in the law of the Lord, and on His law (the precepts, the instructions, the teachings of God) he habitually meditates (ponders and studies) by day and by night.
>
> And he shall be like a tree firmly planted [and tended] by the streams of water, ready to bring forth its fruit in its season; its leaf also shall not fade or wither; and everything he does shall prosper [and come to maturity] (Psalm 1:1-3 AMP).

A firmly planted tree whose roots are established in the love of Christ Jesus, prospering in all that he does is the reward for all those years of nurturing, training, teaching (causing to learn, to enlighten, direct, inform, understand, discern, and instruct), and admonishing (warning based on instruction).

The word "nurturing" in the Greek is the word *paideia,* which means disciplinary correction, chastening, chastisement, and instruction as in Hebrews 12:5-11.[1] It also denotes the training of a child as in Ephesians 6:4:

> Fathers, do not irritate and provoke your children to anger [do not exasperate them to resentment], but rear them [tenderly] in the training and discipline and the counsel and admonition of the Lord.

I've seen parents who don't teach their children, yet they want to punish them for whatever they do wrong. That does not compute—let me repeat—that does not compute with me.

Children are not to teach themselves how to live a godly life in the Lord. Training is our responsibility, and the first ingredient in training is love. With this in mind, can you imagine how much easier it is to train up a child while he or she is really young?

Dez and I started training while our sons were in the womb, as I described in chapter 3. As they grew, we started seeing tiny fruit form. As we taught them more, we saw how the fruit enlarged and increased; they became more loving, more compassionate, more in tune to Holy Spirit—sometimes it seemed like it formed overnight, but not always. While children are fruit of our womb, we must allow the fruit of the Spirit to grow in them over time.

Too often, we want to see fruit in our children instantly produced, but it just does not work like that. Rest assured, though, when we don't see instant manifestations, Holy Spirit is working internally to help bring them about.

The Fruit of Instruction and Discipline

I don't remember disciplining our sons for lying because they knew that we would listen and understand better if they just told the truth. Dezmond and Dominick would end up telling on themselves anyway, which defeated the need to lie. However, Dez has prayed, and still prays, that Holy Spirit would convict our sons' hearts if they are anywhere they're not supposed to be or are doing things they were not taught to do.

Don't get us wrong; they did things they weren't supposed to do, and we did discipline them by taking away privileges to toys (at a young age) or the sports they loved to participate in, and other disciplinary actions. However, Dez would talk to them about their behavior before he disciplined them. He wanted our sons to know that he separated the behavior from the love he had for them. Afterward, he would always hug them and let them know that he loved them; he just did not condone their behavior.

I even remember when Dez wept after one punishment. Even though it's painful for us, sometimes, we have to save our children from themselves so that they will become outstanding citizens, like our Lord. He obeyed the civil authorities (Matthew 17:24-27) and admonished us to do the same (1 Peter 2:13-17, and Romans 13). Discipline is a powerful means to produce that kind of godly action in our children.

As my husband would say, "We are raising young men who need to know love, have the character of our Lord, be diligent, and disciplined." Dez was a military man who also had a tender heart. He always listened and understood from a father's perspective; but when he asked our sons to do something, he meant just that.

Reinforcing Boundaries

It's not only our duty as parents to set boundaries, we must reinforce them. Our children knew their boundaries, such as the curfews that we set to protect them from all the elements in the world (the gangs, drugs, thieves, people with no character or morals, such as white-collar criminals).

If our children broke curfew and Dez promised to ground them for it, he followed through on his word to let them know he meant what he said. Parents, it's okay to set the ground rules and to say *no!* to your children when they want to cross the safety lines.

Dezmond was in his sophomore year of college when Dez decided to buy him a car. The car remained in my husband's name until Dezmond graduated from college. It was a gift, but like Dez says, "I'm raising sons who are going to be responsible, God-fearing, young men." So , while we paid for the car, the insurance, and the maintenance, Dezmond had to keep his curfew. We told him, "If you're going to miss it, please call and let us know where you are and when can we expect you."

Dezmond stuck with the plan. On the other hand (smile), I have my social eagle, and his name is Dominick. He and his brother are cut in Father's design, opposites in personalities, yet they get along so beautifully.

Dominick tried his best to stretch the limit with his boundaries. He would debate us down to the ground to prove his point, and could truly wear us out. One time he broke curfew and tried to explain his way out, but Dez held his line and refused to budge on the issue. As punishment, Dominick had to catch a ride with his dad to campus. Yes, he was grounded! He bucked the status quo a few more times, and while he was talking to his pop about it, I would say to myself, "HOLD that LINE! Do not move because if you let him slide, he'll try it again."

Dez did hold the line, but then Dominick did something we never expected. He was entering his junior year in college when he and one of his friends decided to have a Friday night birthday party at a club. Their birthdays were a week apart, so they wanted to celebrate together. This is one of those times Dez and I were praying and watching.

In Tallahassee, we have two major public universities, one private university, a junior college, and a technical school. One could say we're a college town. Dominick and his friend decided they were going to charge for admission and rent coach tour buses to bus the freshman in, since they didn't have transportation. He had even talked about it with his pastor, the head of the college ministry whom he had known since he was eleven years old. The pastor told him it wasn't a good idea.

Dez and I became aware of their plan a few days before party day. Dez didn't handle the news well, especially when Dominick and his friend started advertising the event on the radio. You have got to understand; Dominick is a very innovative young man. Remember, he is our social eagle. Well, Dez could not understand why he would want a party at a club and, you know me, I trusted that Father can turn anything around for our good—therefore, the intruder was not going to have the first nor the last word on how this party was going to turn out.

In all cases, I always try to get the strategy of the Lord. As I prayed, Holy Spirit gave me an idea. I called Living Waters ministry in California, who are very strong in evangelism support; they have unusual tracts for handing out to unsaved souls. Some of them look like real million dollar bills, and if you look closely, the gospel message is printed on the back. I ordered the tracts on a Tuesday and received them Thursday.

We were armed and ready to go. I gave the plan to Dez, Dezmond, D. Jerome, and Courtney (family friends). As the students came out of the bus, we introduced ourselves, handed them the tracts, told them that they were party favors, and to not open them until they got back to their dorms or apartments.

We also handed them to the students lined up and ready to go into the club. One of the young men really thought we were handing out money. He read it and said, "Cool," and put it into his pocket. He seemed to stop and ponder it before he moved up in line. If even one of them received the message, went home and thought about it enough to ask questions and look in the Word for answers, then that was enough for me. Some plant, some water, but it is God who causes the growth and gets the increase (1 Corinthians 3: 5-9).

Dez and I went to eat breakfast and came back to the club just before the party ended. We made sure Dominick let all the ladies board the buses first (he had already started doing that before we arrived). We didn't get home until four in the morning.

A couple of days later, Dominick asked his pop, "What are we going to do for my birthday?"

"Nothing," he said. We always celebrate birthdays as special events in the family. So Dez told him, "Since you wanted to celebrate your birthday without including us, we're not going to celebrate it."

Dominick has always had a mind of his own, but when Holy Spirit speaks to him, he apologizes from his heart. He knew his pop was hurt, and oh how he fell into his arms, cried, and asked for his pop's forgiveness. And he got it. Our sons do not like for us to be disappointed in them.

Just as our Father restores us to sonship when we stretch our boundaries, so should we as parents restore our children when they do things that go against what we have taught them.

The Fruit of Self-Respect

Your child is just as good as everyone else--not better or worse, so sometimes we have to protect their dignity and self-respect and say no for them, especially when they're young.

When Dezmond was about nine years old, he really wanted to go to a friend's birthday party, but he was the only boy not invited out of his age group until, finally, on the day of the party, the birthday child invited him.

His Pop and I said, "You will not go. Absolutely not!"

Dez wept and was so filled with emotion as he hugged Dezmond tight. He told Dezmond that he (Dez) did not go through certain things in his childhood for his son to be treated like a second-class citizen. It was difficult for Dezmond to understand; all he knew was that he wanted to go to the party. It was the quietest moment in my life, and as my mother used to say, "You could not hear a rat urinate on cotton." It was that quiet.

We not only taught our sons to respect their dignity but also their bodies and the bodies of others. Father does not have double standards! What He meant for one, He meant for all. What is great for your daughters, is also great for your sons. So I asked my sons a question; I know they thought that I was crazy but I was serious. I asked, "If a prostitute came up to you and offered you sex, what would you do?"

They were astonished to hear me ask that, so I gave them mom's take on the answer. I said to them, "You've been reading and meditating on Proverbs for years, so let me go further in expounding on the warnings about loose women in the Book of Proverbs."

I saw that I got their attention, so I continued. "There are a lot of hurt ladies in the world that have been raped, been victims of incest, are fatherless (looking for daddy in all the wrong places), have been involved in sex trafficking against their will, and the list goes on. Don't you think God loves them and frowns on what has happened to them? As a matter of fact, He hates it!"

They remained attentive because they knew I wasn't playing with them; our sons do know their mother. I went on to say, "Your place is not to be taken in by her vice. Instead, be like our Lord (Luke 7:36-39; John 4:7-29, and John 8) and help her to see Him in you. Think of her as a lost child who has incurred hidden trauma in her life."

They understood so well that when I started to repeat it any time after that, they'd say, " We know mom."

There is so much to be said on this subject, but let me say again that our God is not double-minded. I can't find anywhere in the Word where it says, "Daughters, stay pure; sons, get all you can, sit on the can, and oh don't forget to find a virgin when you get married." Too many young ladies have been messed up by this kind of double-mindedness. Instead the word says,

> Treat younger men like brothers, older women like mothers and younger women like sisters, with absolute purity (1 Timothy 5:1-2 CJB).

Can you imagine if every young male were taught what is right in the sight of the Lord? Think about how it would affect the number of rapes and other sexual crimes in America alone. There would be no human trafficking, and no prostitutes because every man would be thinking about restoring everyone (males and females) to their rightful place in the Lord. They would behave as Paul asked his spiritual child, Timothy, to behave:

> Don't let anyone look down on you because of your youth; on the contrary, set the believers an

> example in your speech, behavior, love, trust and purity (1 Timothy 4:12 CJB). "

I pray this book has such an effect on you, especially you who have sons. I want to stress the point again that our Father is not double-minded on any subject, especially sexual promiscuity. That young lady in pain is Father's spiritual daughter and someone's natural daughter; shouldn't she be allowed to let Him clean her up?

Fruit That Remains

One day, Dezmond and I were talking about having a close relationship with the Lord and how one generation affects the next one. We also discussed how the Lord looks at purity of heart and sexual purity. Dezmond chimed in saying, "I know Mom, because I carry generations in my loins."

I was taken aback, but realized the truth of his statement. God is the God of Abraham, Isaac, and Jacob (Israel). There is such an urgent need for us as parents to realize how each generation interlocks to form a straight path for the future generations to walk on. When one generation repents (changes its direction and walks the Lord's way), they in turn, teach their children to walk the Lord's way; then, the third generation will also taste and see that the Lord is good, and so on and so on. Every generation should give its children something to build upon; no generation should have to start at the beginning.

I constantly remind our sons, "Father wants you to excel spiritually in Him so that you'll excel in the natural. That will cause every generation after you to be better than the last one."

That's why it's so important to teach our sons and daughters to think about their children when they make decisions on how to live their lives. We have the Word of the Lord on it, and the Word has always and will always yield great increase.

> How shall a young man cleanse his way? By taking heed and keeping watch [on himself] according to Your word [conforming his life to it]. With my whole heart have I sought You, inquiring for and of You and yearning for You; Oh, let me not wander or step aside [either in ignorance or willfully] from Your commandments (Psalm 119:9-10).

Closing Thoughts

Today, I'm sitting at the table eating breakfast with my husband and sons. It's Father's Day 2011. We are all reminded to celebrate the Father of all fathers first and foremost. Then Dominick began to tell his pop how much he and Dezmond appreciated us staying in love; they shared how that has been a mainstay in their lives.

My mind went back in time and I remembered all the things Holy Spirit had taught us concerning them. Tears fell from my eyes as I looked at Dez, and we nodded our heads at each other. So many interactions like this with our sons have given us evidence that parenting *His Precious Cargo* by Holy Spirit bears fruit upon fruit, upon fruit, upon fruit.

That old African proverb: "When you walk in the path of your Father, you learn to walk like Him" is so true. I don't know if they meant the Father, but I do because a good father points to the Father.

Jesus walked the path of His Father (John 14 and 17), and He challenges all of us to walk it, too. He challenged Dez who didn't have a father in his household. It's amazing to see how he has grasped the Lord's wisdom, understanding, and knowledge in fatherhood. He is a natural at it, and that is a gift from God. Father taught him well.

Dez strived to teach his children to walk the path of the Lord so they will be established (rooted and grounded) in Him to do whatever are in His plans for them wherever He calls them.

Are they now perfect?

Absolutely not!

Do they have a spirit of excellence?

Yes!

Is there a difference?

Yes!

There is only One who is perfect—our Lord God, Jesus the Christ, Yeshua, our Messiah.

Dez and I don't seek perfection from our sons. Instead, we set out to raise sons in the nurture and admonition of the Lord so that they will become men of excellence, men who will be an asset to the Kingdom of God, therefore, an asset to society. In doing so, we have left an inheritance—a bushel of fruit—for our children's children of much more than money and personal possessions.

What kind of fruit will you leave your Precious Cargo?

Let us pray:

FATHER, in the name of Jesus, I thank you for parents who will stay committed to raising their children, your sons and daughters, until the fruit starts to appear and long after.

I thank You that they will continue their prayers for their children as long as breath is in them and that they have not ceased to pray and make [special] request for their children, [asking] that you may be filled with the full (deep and clear) knowledge of His will in all spiritual wisdom [incomprehensive insight into the ways and purposes of God] and in understanding and discernment of spiritual things—

That their children may walk (live and conduct themselves) in a manner worthy of the Lord, fully pleasing to Him and desiring to please Him in all things, bearing fruit in every good work and steadily growing and increasing in and by the knowledge of God [with fuller, deeper, and clearer insight, acquaintance, and recognition].

~ Adapted from Colossians 1:9-10

But you, continue in what you have learned and have become convinced of, recalling the people from whom you learned it; and recalling too how from childhood you have known the Holy Scriptures, which can give you the wisdom that leads to deliverance through trusting in Yeshua the Messiah.

~ 2 Timothy 3:14-15 CJB

Nothing gives me greater joy
than hearing that my children
are living in the truth.
~ 3 John 4 CJB

The Fruit Speaks

I shared with you the personal and professional outcome of our twins, Joshua and Jacob. Now I want to tell you about Dezmond and Dominick's journey.

We were ecstatic that they wanted to go to college, but I want to stress that their success rests in their relationship with Father through our Messiah Christ Jesus. They know how to tune in to Father's voice, how to praise the Lord without a praise and worship leader, how to pray and touch the Father's heart by being a prayer warrior for so many others, how to discern correctly through love; and they know how to meditate on the Word, as they listen and obey the Spirit of the Living God.

Dez and I thank Father all the time for His Grace poured out upon our sons and ourselves. School, like so many other things in life, are but a by-product of the love relationship between them and God. When they reach college age, your children need to hear from God for themselves and not from you as parents. This is the parent's time to step back, but to still keep praying concerning the decisions they make. Be available when they want to communicate, so that you can establish a new kind of relationship with your sons and daughters (a deeper friendship). Even today our sons discuss matters of life, work, school, and heart with us, and all I can say is, "Thank you, Father."

Our sons love to hear from Holy Spirit for themselves. They have been given strong prophetic words concerning their purpose, calling, and destiny, and we are persuaded that Father is bringing it forth.

Dezmond graduated with his B.S. in Mathematics and worked for about two years while he pondered (having a fixed propensity and determined resolve) what his purpose in life was. He's now working on his master's degree in Architecture (the art of building). We noticed his love of design and form even when he played with all the building sets we used to buy for him as presents. More importantly, he's a builder of people in the spiritual realm as well as in the natural.

Throughout college in Tallahassee, Dezmond worked as a tutor (math and science) for high school students enrolled in the SSTRIDE Program (Students Striving Together Reaching Individual Diversity and Excellence), the same program he and his brothers were a part of. We call him our "gentle giant" because he stands tall in the wisdom of God and His Word.

Dominick graduated with his B.S. in Health Care Management and is pursuing his dual master's degrees in International Affairs and Urban Planning; that's the essence of who he is with regard to his purpose in life. He loves interacting with people, is very gifted in music, and has a keen sensitivity to Holy Spirit.

Dezmond and Dominick both received Florida Bright Futures Scholarships when they graduated from high school and Dominick received one other scholarship while he was working on his B.S. Degree. Dezmond had an academic scholarship at a private Christian University in Oklahoma, which he attended his freshman year; this is where we met Abraham (Abe) Perez, Kason Oakes, and Yuri Battle.

These three young men had integrity and a zeal for the purpose of God in their lives. Their parents had taken time to really raise them correctly. Abe and Yuri were juniors at the time, and Kason and Dezmond were freshmen. Kason was from Oklahoma so they used to go to his home once every six weeks or so for his mother's and grandmother's cooking, and to see if Dezmond's hair was long enough for Kason's mother to braid (smile).

Abe is from Puerto Rico, and Yuri is from California. Yuri wrote Dez and I this beautiful letter below in 2002. I kept it because it is so special to me. He was a blessing to Dezmond and continues to speak encouragement to him. Thank you, Yuri, for being who you are. You've represented God and your parents well!

Hello Mr. & Mrs. Ard'is,

I just would like to thank you very much for sending me the gifts. I really appreciated them (cookies and phone card). The phone card really came in handy in calling home or attempting to attain scholarships, or even calling loved ones back home and in school as well.

Dezmond is doing well at school, as you may very well already know. He is definitely assuming a leadership position here on the floor as well. His desire for following God is uncontrollably changing all of our lives. What am I saying? That in watching him, some of us on the floor have already done some detailed "soul searching" of ourselves to make sure that we are indeed walking with the Heavenly Father. But having Dezmond here has truly blessed my life. I want to thank you for supporting his decision in coming here.

When I first met you all back in August (Mom, Dad, and Brother). I knew that you all were all about God's business and the advancement of His Kingdom. I was sure that this would be a semester full of God's excellence and favor. And let me tell you it was truly that ☺. I thoroughly enjoy Dezmond's company as well as his insight on the Word.

I just thank God for parents like yourselves who step in bless others, sometimes times are hard and we need to hear from others to "hang in there and keep on praying". You don't see that a lot around here (shocking I know), but it is true. Some parents could care less about how there kids are doing in school. That is not the case in the Ard'is Household.

May God bless you all and thank you for the gifts.

Sincerely,

Yurrennis L. Battle

Yuri is now married (Dezmond was one of his groomsmen) to a beautiful lady (Shalondra) and has two handsome sons Elijah James (4), and Matthew Lashon (2) and lives in Oklahoma. He received his B.S. from Oral Roberts University and is pursuing his master's degree in Education while working at State Farm as a fire underwriter.

Another "child" of mine is Michele Freilich Paske. She's my Messianic Jewish baby girl who taught me a lot about the Jewish faith. I've watched her grow into a beautiful young lady with a bubbly personality that is so contagious. She got married one year ago and is blissfully happy. I know she and her husband are married "for keeps."

Dear Momma,

You are a prayer warrior and mighty woman of God standing in the gap for many, diligently believing we will fulfill the Lord's plans. Thank you for believing in me encouraging me to come out my shell & overcome my past. A good momma is hard to find and a rare treasure far more precious than rubies. You are one of those priceless gems shining the light of Messiah. That is a quality I have looked for in a mom.

Thank you for your covenant love and care. May your cup continue to run over with the Fruit of the Spirit so that all men & women will be drawn unto the Lord.

In His Grace & Love,

Eph 2:10

Michelle

We've known Brett Thomas for ten plus years. He's one of Dominick's inner circle friends; he's a part of our family and is living his life for the Lord. He received his B.S. in Biology from the University of Florida and is now attending medical school at Florida State University. He wants to become a physician who is filled with the Great Physician. God bless and keep you Brett, you truly are a blessing to Dominick! It has been a true blessing for us to see you grow in the integrity of the Lord. Thank you for your letter:

Dear Mr. and Mrs. Ard'is,

There is no doubt that our acquaintance was orchestrated divinely. Our Heavenly Father knew I would need spiritual parental figures in the process of me coming to know my beautiful Savior. I remember the days of visiting Dominick and Desmond in Arbor View apartments. Although I knew the prerequisite to going outside to play was an hour long "heart to heart" talk (and most kids wanted to evade it) it was comforting to know that you cared about me and my life. There was a peaceful atmosphere in your home; I felt like I could be my broken self without judgment and/or commendation passed. It was a home of unconditional love, comparable to what Jesus feels for me. Even though I had my period of time in college where I ran from you and the Lord, you were the family I knew I could come to for support, love, and direction. You were the family that stood boldly with me when I broke the agreement with fraternal involvement and other lies. You were the family that let me know you were proud of me and encouraged me in the Faith. For this, I am forever grateful. I can honestly say that I've learned what the family and the Church looks like based on my relationship with you. I pray that Holy Spirit continues to shape you more into the image of the Son and your hearts grow in love. You are truly making a difference in the lives of young people and in my own life.

Forever in my prayers and heart,

Brett Thomas

Brett A. Thomas

Medical Student, Class of 2014, Florida State University College of Medicine

Student Body President

Service Coordinator, Christian Medical and Dental Association

D. Jerome Garrett is special to our family. We have loved him as a son, teacher, mentor, and big brother. He and his wife Janice, also a teacher, have graced our family and table many a time. They know what it is to be family in the Kingdom of God, and to extend themselves in their multiple gifting and talents to God's people.

May Father continue to bless and keep you in Christ Jesus.

The authentication of the tree is the taste of its fruit. Mr. & Mrs. Ardis are such precious jewels to the Body of Christ, as well as, rare and special gifts to the world. They are indeed an Apostolic Father and Mother; as evident, I have seen them unselfishly give of their time, talent, and treasure to be a blessing to so many people. I am honored to speak as a spiritual son, just one of the many fruit of their labor of love. I met them in 1995, sixteen years ago, and their sons: Dezmond and Dominick were students at Metropolitan Christian Academy of the Arts, the same school where I was a teacher. Immediately, I was able to identify the excellence, the spark, the edge, and the anointing that they had on their lives, as they worked and played with their peers. Consequently, like night and day, Dezmond and Dominick were very intelligent and very well behaved. With great anticipation, I looked forward to meeting their parents. After meeting Mr. & Mrs. Ardis, they unconditionally loved and accepted me as a part of their extended family. They have been very supportive in my personal development, marriage and ministry. Later, I became a mentor to their sons, and it has been a privileged to see them matriculate from grammar school to graduate school. What can I say? The proof is in the pudding. Therefore, I am excited about the release of **"Precious Cargo."** I know it is going to be a continual blessing to the generations and the nations.

D. Jerome Garrett

D, Jerome Garrett, Founder & Pastor
Covenant Restoration International Inc. and
Creative Child Solutions LLC

Notes

Author's Message

1. Paraphrased from *New Strongs Expanded Dictionary of Bible Words* (2001) s.v. "yada"

Introduction

1. *New Strongs Expanded Dictionary of Bible Words* (2001) s.v. "yaqar"
2. *Webster's 1828 American Dictionary of the English Language,* s.v. "cargo"
3. *Webster's 1828,* s.v. "charge"
4. Paraphrased from *New Strongs,* s.v. "chanak"
5. *Webster's 1828,* s.v. "selfishness"
6. *Webster's 1828,* s.v. "covenant"
7. Paraphrased from *New Strongs,* s.v. "tsavah"

Chapter Two

1. *Webster's 1828,* s.v. "pray"
2. *Webster's 1828,* s.v. "prayer"
3. *New Strongs,* s.v. "ânnâ"
4. *New Strongs,* s.v. "proseuchomai"
5. Paraphrased from *New Strongs,* s.v. "barak"
6. Paraphrased from *New Strongs,* s.v. "shalowm"
7. Paraphrased from *New Strongs,* s.v. "sakal"

Chapter Seven

1. Paraphrased from *New Strongs,* s.v. "paideia"

www.ingramcontent.com/pod-product-compliance
Lightning Source LLC
LaVergne TN
LVHW091004080826
845145LV00003B/1122

* 9 7 8 0 9 8 5 2 0 0 7 0 1 *